How to Believe Again

by the same author

BETWEEN HEAVEN AND EARTH
CHRIST AND THE MEANING OF LIFE
ENCOUNTER WITH SPURGEON
ETHICS OF SEX
HOW MODERN SHOULD THEOLOGY BE?
HOW THE WORLD BEGAN
I BELIEVE
LIFE CAN BEGIN AGAIN
MAN IN GOD'S WORLD
NIHILISM
THE PRAYER THAT SPANS THE WORLD
THEOLOGICAL ETHICS
THE TROUBLE WITH THE CHURCH
THE WAITING FATHER

How to Believe Again

Helmut Thielicke

TRANSLATED BY H. GEORGE ANDERSON

FORTRESS PRESS

PHILADELPHIA

Library of Congress Catalog Card Number 72-75656

ISBN 0-8006-0123-8

3230H72   1-123

CONTENTS

48261

BETTING ON GOD:
A WORD TO THE READER

In the following chapters I address myself principally to those of my contemporaries for whom "God" is an open question. If one doesn't know who God is, or even *if* God is, one is naturally puzzled by people who claim to believe in God and who literally bet their lives on him.

I have always been especially interested in these particular contemporaries. Both my life and my profession have brought me more contact with them than with specifically Christian circles. Many are friends of mine. With many of them I have repeatedly had searching conversations on the "God question."

Normally it is not because of any missionary zeal on my part that such dialogues occur. Usually it is my partners in conversation who themselves introduce the subject. Often they start out with something like, "We have the feeling that you are one of us. You are fun to talk to and you enjoy a good joke. We don't smell any fire and brimstone. But how in the world can a person with a critical mind believe in God and associate with people who are highly suspect from our point of view?" I have used a stylized form to describe these conversations because the questions are naturally posed in widely varied ways—often quite obliquely. In content, however, the quotation is exact.

I can always distinguish two types of people among those who thus express their bewilderment: One group consists of those who simply have a certain human interest in the person with whom they are speaking—in this case, poor old me. For a Christian, and especially a theologian, to have both his feet pretty firmly on the ground and to refuse to let anyone pull the wool over his eyes is an enigma to them, a comic mixture of intelligence and superstition. It arouses their psychological curiosity. The God question, however, although it is involved, has no interest for them. They consider it settled.

For my part, however, I am far from uninterested in such indifferent people. If I want to take God seriously, these people concern me for *his* sake because, among all that the Bible says about him, one thing definitely stands out: God is not simply the leader of his own earthly followers. (That would be very damaging for him, since many who are considered "very religious" or "his" because they are good church members would be much more likely to compromise his cause than to make it more attractive.) No, God isn't kept alive by his followers. He is the God of the atheists too. He remains true, even when men disavow him.

For that reason I often watched like a hawk for opportunities to say something along that line to people who had no time for God. I seldom did it through argument or intellectual fencing (of course that does occur, but it usually doesn't get very far). I simply told them a "Bible story." After all, God becomes believable to us only through what he does, and through the people who are involved in that action. When I spoke like that, people pricked up their ears. And even when they shook their heads, I thought I could see traces of wistfulness and now and then even a sense of amazement.

This book, however, is not chiefly directed to these indifferent people. That is not because I have given up on them, but because I doubt that they will even read a book of this sort. A Marxist like Vitezslav Gardavsky will have a better chance of reaching them when they hear him support the thesis that God is "not quite dead" yet and that one must read the Bible "if one does not want to be poorer than other men." Since God is a God of the atheists, he not only has regular troops who are loyal to him, but also guerrillas.

At any rate I have directed the following pages more toward the second group among those who are surprised to find people like me believing in God.

Their astonishment contains a note for which a man in my profession develops a sensitive ear. This note may most easily be described by means of a question that I draw out of that astonishment. Unfolded in a rambling monologue, it goes something like this: "I am far removed from everything that has to do with God (to say nothing of Christ), with faith, and with religion. I am like Faust on Easter eve when, just as he is about to drink the poison to 'flee into nothingness,' he hears the bells ring and a choir singing. That's as close as I get to religion. But what good are those mellow feelings which the bells arouse in me? I hear the message all right, I just lack the faith. Yet should we want the sort of faith that arises out of a mere concession to our emotions? And yet I ask myself, 'What if there is something to it?' I can't get away from that question. I dimly perceive that the basis, goal, and meaning of my life would look completely different, depending on whether or not I took God into consideration.

"Naturally I am not stupid enough to assume that if I believed in God all my problems would be solved and everything would make sense—including all the riddles of my life and of history in general. Even though an expert pilot stood at the helm of the universe and I as an insignificant passenger could confidently entrust myself to his course—that doesn't mean that ultimately nothing could ever go wrong. I well know that it is not that simple. I notice that those of my friends who have been given the ability to believe are not that simple and naïve either. They too may have to traverse the dark stretches of doubt, anxious care and disappointed hopes. But they finally make it through. Even when they don't understand the strange 'higher thoughts' (Isa. 55:9) that are thought about them, they still share in the fact of those thoughts and the security they provide. An absolutely meaningless world *without* 'higher thoughts' is worse by far.

"And I confess openly, albeit somewhat reluctantly, that I have never quite understood Camus's efforts to wrest a positive and creative side out of the absurdity of a Sisyphus-like existence. As far as I am concerned, if I had to believe that everything was meaningless and that there was no 'theme' for my life or for others, then there would be no more joy in life. It would bore me to see flowers bloom in the spring and then fade away. History would seem an 'eternal creating, sweeping away what had been created before'—moving, but never getting anywhere. When cancer claimed a loved one, it would simply

9

be an extreme indication of that general senselessness. From this point of view I can understand the words of the 'dead Christ' in Jean Paul's *Siebenkäs*: 'Frozen, mute Nothingness! Cold, eternal Necessity! Crazy Coincidence! Do you know what's happening? When are you going to destroy the city and me?'

"Everything would be different, though, if it were possible for me to believe that God is. Then I wouldn't need to torment myself with the question—which often comes to me when I have had a little success in my business—what good is it? What lasting difference does it make? And what will become of me when I get older and can't stand the strain any more? *If* God is, then I could be certain that all the various chapters of my life 'hung together'—that they had a meaningful connection with each other, even though I didn't recognize it. The Author of that story, however, would have opened his heart to me so that I could entrust myself completely to him. I think that would be plenty; that would be more than enough. But I don't get that far. And if I try nonetheless, I begin to ask myself whether I'm giving in to a cowardly illusion. Could it be that I am a defeatist, who is unable to bear the agony of meaninglessness, and therefore seeks to escape into the never-never land of empty consolation?"

This long monologue, like the earlier conversation, is a stylized composition which I have woven together out of many individual remarks. But it is interesting to note how all these comments and expressions move in an ellipse around two foci.

One of these focal points is the knowledge that God is inconceivably far removed from us and that to believe in him is more than I can manage.

The second focus is only a hunch: an undefined feeling that my fate nevertheless depends on this most complete Uncertainty. The affirmation or denial that takes place here will decide the realities of my life, its loves and hates, its hopes and fears, its anxieties and its assurances. How annoying, though, that precisely the most important thing in life cannot be calculated! How paradoxical that, although I can determine profit and loss on my account books down to the last penny, when it comes to summing up the *totality* of my life the decisive entry will have to be an unknown X! If that is the case, aren't we humans in an odd and downright crazy situation?

Ultimately it all seems to culminate in this issue: If the God question actually assumes such a key role in summing up our life, why doesn't God provide us with arguments or indications that would make us conscious of his presence? Isn't this hiddenness refutation enough? Yet without him things don't work out either.

How do we get out of this strange situation? Put another way, how do we proceed in face of the question, "And if there be a God . . . ?"

The only way I know is the one recommended by Pascal in a very bold chapter of his *Pensées*. The chapter is called "The Wager." It is about a conversation with a prominent, well-educated man of the world, an "honest man," who belongs to the second group of doubters that I described above. He is a man who cannot believe and yet does not consider himself ready simply to lay his faith aside, and tell himself, "I prefer to hang on to the concrete certainties of my daily life. I drain my existence and see what I get out of it. That way metaphysical uncertainties—above all the question of whether God is or is not—won't bother me." He cannot take that way out. He cannot shake off the upsetting possibility that lurks beneath the question, "And if there be a God—what then?"

Perhaps he thinks, "This Pascal with his mathematically trained mind must certainly have reasons for believing in God. A man of his intellectual caliber is just incapable of doing things *without* reasons. If only he would share his arguments with me. I'll put myself in his hands."

In other words, he wants a rational test in the case of the God question. At first he seems to receive a rebuke. The crossword puzzle "God" remains rationally insolvable. Pascal lets him know that "according to reason, you can do neither the one thing nor the other (that is, decide whether God is or is not); according to reason, you can defend neither of the propositions."[1] Therefore—this is the conclusion which Pascal draws—

1. Pascal, *Pensées*, trans. W. F. Trotter, Modern Library (1941), 164; 81.

one must "choose." A choice of this sort is made in the form of a decision that is full of risk precisely because it cannot be calculated rationally. To that extent it is like a bet. When you go to a bookmaker to put money on a horse or a football team, you usually follow certain rational leads in determining which way to bet. You may have checked the previous record of the horse or the team; you coolly balance the estimated effect of training and present condition. Yet all of these leads still leave wide latitude for imponderables and unknown factors. No way of calculating can include all the variables. Therefore betting necessarily involves a risk. Instead of taking a rational step, I must do something totally different. I must make a leap.

It is exactly the same with God. There is a risk involved in choosing him. I must bet.

Pascal's hearer is shocked at this answer. It is no more obvious to him than it is to us that the fundamental question of our life is to be decided by a bet—and therefore made subject to the happenstance of choice. His resistance to this idea of a bet expresses itself in tough counterarguments. I don't need to go into them here nor into Pascal's incisive replies. It is enough at this point to take note of the preliminary conclusion to which the controversy over God's existence or nonexistence has brought us. This conclusion can be detected in the resigned observation of Pascal's companion: "Yes, but I have my hands tied and my mouth closed; I am forced to wager, and am not free . . . and am so made that I cannot believe. What, then, would you have me to do?"[2]

Thus far the conversation has led into a blind alley. Now Pascal wants to provide us with a way out—a way that may appear quite strange to us. He tells that man of the world sitting across from him who has no faith (I am simply giving the gist of what he said), "You don't get anywhere by seeking proofs for God, because the range of your mind just won't reach that far. It's your passions that must be brought under control. Your reason isn't what is hindering you from finding a clear answer to the question of God. In this matter reason is not capable of pronouncing a valid yes or a valid no. Your limita-

2. Pascal, *Pensées*, p. 83.

tions stem from an entirely different dimension of your ego. They come from your passions."

Immediately the question arises as to whether this suggestion doesn't switch the God question to a *moral* track. That would be almost macabre. One is strongly tempted to greet this diversionary tactic with a wry smile and to get a little provoked.

Doesn't an approach like that, after all, amount to nothing more than the silly advice, "Just be a paragon of virtue and the religious convictions will take care of themselves"?

Yet the matter is not that simple.

A later passage in this same chapter on the God question makes clear that Pascal is referring to a dimension of our ego which lies deep beneath the level of morality. In it he turns his attention to unbelievers in general, to the personality "type" which dominates in such cases, revealing certain basic character-istics as a sort of constant in all forms of unbelief. " 'I would soon have renounced pleasure,' they say, 'had I faith.' For my part I tell you, 'You would soon have faith, if you would quickly have renounced pleasure.' "[3]

At first glance this observation of Pascal's seems to play right into the hands of a somewhat narrow-eyed morality. I need to make a couple of comments about it.

The people that Pascal is talking about are shrewd in a subtle sort of way. The mental chess game by which they intend to checkmate belief in God is planned as follows.

To begin with they must be pictured as people who enjoy life to the full with supreme and perhaps even gross indulgence, and who want to develop their personalities completely. Indeed, without exaggeration, they may be called hedonists who seek the joy of self-fulfillment. In the midst of this rich, full life there is only one disturbing element that detracts from their un-interrupted pleasure. That is their conscience. No matter how pleasant something is, when I do it with a bad conscience the pleasure is considerably diminished. That we all know! To stumble over a taboo in the midst of enjoyment is like a killing frost on a spring night. A bad conscience is a pain which denies the enjoyment of life. And when this enjoyment becomes the

3. Pascal, *Pensées*, p. 85.

supreme standard, then everything depends on eliminating that disturbing pain.

But how can that be done?

The thing that disturbs one so is the unconditional "thou shalt" and "thou shalt not" of conscience. But it is none other than God, the Author of all commandments, who makes himself heard in this claim of "shall." The taproot of this disturbing element that hinders my unrestrained pleasure runs back to God. If I am able to tear myself away from this root or to convince myself it does not exist, then at one stroke I am free from the pain of a bad conscience.

The train of thought of unbelievers begins from such a calculation. They want Pascal, the mathematical genius and philosophical sage, to turn state's evidence and prove that God is not a reality with whom one needs to deal. Then He would not need to disturb them in the springtime of their sins. So they come to him with the innocent-sounding request, "Dear Pascal, present us with a proof of God and then we will give up our dissipation."

They are really anxious to appear as people who are serious about the matter and who are ready to accept the consequences, whatever they turn out to be. If they were to become convinced that there was a God, then they would lay the axe to the root of their former existence. They are ready to take extreme measures.

The pattern of their thought is: First we want theoretical clarity, then we are ready to draw the practical consequences. We really are!

Their theory is, in fact, quite shrewd. For as educated people they are well aware that there *is* no proof for God (and indeed for very serious and understandable reasons which have to do with God's being). Therefore they can rightly count on Pascal being unable to meet their bid for a proof of God. He will have to pass.

They then calculate further and say to themselves: "In any case what we enjoy are tangible things that we can feel, see, smell, and taste with our senses every day. On the other hand, the disturbing element 'God,' which always spoils this fun of ours, is *not* tangible. Not even a thinker of Pascal's caliber can tell us anything conclusive about him. Why, then, should we let an uncertain metaphysical entity set us against a direct certainty? Isn't a sparrow in the hand—that is, our tasty, tangible pleasure—worth more than a God-dove on the roof? In fact, it isn't even on the roof, because then we would see it! According to some dubious rumor, it is supposed to be floating around somewhere in space. Thus we could go our way unmolested, without having our composure disturbed by a God who was forever plaguing us with interruptions on the intercom called 'conscience.' "

Pascal has obviously seen through their little game and guards himself against being taken in by their tactics. In fact, he turns their guns back upon them and counterattacks: "You've miscalculated," he informs them. "It is just not possible to achieve some sort of objective clarity about the existence of God in peace and quiet, and then afterward to draw the practical consequences and change your way of life. It is precisely the other way around. First change your life; then you will discover God!"

Is it clear to us that Pascal wants to get at something far more fundamental than a pious moral cliché? He unfolds an apparently moralistic argument in order to point out two things.

He says, first, to these intellectuals and hedonists that God cannot be had cheaply—by a mere spectator without involvement. On the contrary, one must get into the game. Whoever is not ready to sell all that he has will—if there be a God—never get to see him.

And secondly, Pascal tells these people: "Our rational arguments are always decided by fear and hope—that is, by personal interests. (That is the case, at any rate, insofar as our rationality deals with matters outside the exact natural sciences.) Isn't the proverb right when it says that the man is father to his thoughts? What we want, we gladly believe—we even 'think' it gladly! Ideologies are a good example of the degree to which our wishes can become the driving force behind our thought processes. The same thing is true of our fears. Our thoughts tend to find reasons, or even to make them

15

up, in order to prove that there are no grounds for those fears. That is the reason that even great surgeons have not recognized their own cancer. When shown the biopsy, their ability to associate ideas—that is, their highly developed medical understanding—has helped them to explain *away* the diseased tissue structure. In other words, our arguments are deeply influenced by our interests—our interests that something come out a certain way or *not* a certain way."

Applied to Pascal's partner in dialogue, that means: "It is to your interest that God *not* exist. Your rich, full life finds him a disturbing element. Therefore, you wish to shove him aside so that you may more completely enjoy your sins while they are in full bloom. Even if I came to you with a proof for God, this private interest of yours would come out with a steady 'Yes, but . . .' You dare not admit to God's existence! You have (like the heathen in Romans 1:18 ff.) 'by . . . wickedness . . . suppressed the truth.' In psychoanalytic terms, you have repressed it. It is not arguments that stand between you and God that in the final analysis cause your unbelief. It is the total attitude of your existence that turns you away from him. This attitude forces you to look in the opposite direction, so that—logically—you can see only the No-God."

After this interlude we return to the noble man of the world whose unbelief caused him to question Pascal. We can now presume that his crisis of faith arises from the same diseased area that affected his intellectual brethren. It is likely that he too has placed himself in a position where he merely debates with Pascal in order to force him to give up and say, "I cannot prove to you by means of arguments that God exists." If that happened, he would at least be relieved of the restlessness which had previously disturbed his unbelief.

But Pascal doesn't let his partner escape that easily. For now his challenge to a bet takes on a new and deeper meaning. At first it seemed as though the bet simply involved a determination to wager blindly for highly risky stakes. But Pascal intends something quite different from a mere turn at the dice, with the result left purely to chance.

What, then, *must* we wager in this question about God, this bet on his existence? Why, precisely the thing that seems to prevent us from seeking him with utter seriousness. What hinders us, says Pascal, is our "passions." In saying that, naturally, he is not advocating as his ideal human being the even-tempered, emotionally restrained (or even "castrated") Mr Average Citizen who never lets the mask fall. The word "passions" in this context is used to express the passion of my own self-will—my self-fulfillment, the draining of all delights to the dregs, the tasting of all the possibilities that mind and nature can present. Certainly not only the inferior enjoyments, but also the self-embodiment of man in his culture—including the sublimest unfolding of his inner being.

My "passion" pushes me toward self-will. I possess "myself," however, only if no one else meddles with me. I need passionately to seek my own undisturbed and autonomous identity. In this sense, therefore, it is not enough for me to stake my *passions* when I bet on God. I must stake myself.

But what does that involve?

As answer I again cite a couple of sentences out of our dialogue. Hopefully, no one will be put out if these sentences have a slightly Catholic ring. Once the essential point that Pascal wants to make is grasped, the unimportant details need not disturb us. He gives the following advice: Follow the way in which all believers once took their first step from unbelief to faith, "by acting as if they believed, taking the holy water, having masses said, etc. Even this will naturally make you believe, and deaden your acuteness."[4]

Pascal means that, if a person learns to bring God into the picture and therefore begins to believe, then he ceases to be so passionately self-willed. Looking back, he discovers that it was this very autonomy, this centering his life on his own ego, that made him seek unbelief and made him fear that faith would threaten his self-will. This and nothing else creates my real inhibition about dealing with the question of God's existence. For it is precisely my self-will that I must put on the line when I wager on God.

According to Pascal, however, these stakes do not involve a

4. Pascal, *Pensées*, p. 83.

H.B.A.—B   17 great risk. *Either* God wins the game, becoming a certainty to me and subduing my unbelief—in which case I am overjoyed with my newfound truth, I experience fulfillment (passionately), and moreover I gain myself back—*or* God loses. He, then, is just as obscure as ever or even becomes known in his nonexistence. Then everything remains as it was. Perhaps I am a little more at peace than before. At least I lost nothing by making the bet.

Yet the question must again be put: What does it mean to put your passions on the line when you bet on God? In simple terms, it means that I carry out an experiment with God. I act temporarily and tentatively "as if" God existed. To act as if God existed means that I "play" the role of a believer. I behave toward my neighbor "as if" the word of God about loving your neighbor as yourself was really in effect. I deal with my cares "as if" someone were there on whom I could cast them. I forgive my fellow man "as if" God forgave me and I had to hand on the gift I had received. I pray "as if" God were there to hear me.

That means I do not wait until I receive some sort of mystical divine revelation, and then, with that evidence as a basis, declare myself ready to live and act in his name. The exact opposite is true. I act tentatively and experimentally in his name, in the name of an *X*, whose being and existence are still an enigma to me. Temporarily I hand my passions over to him —"as if" he existed. To that extent I am putting my self-will on the line and thus they really become the "stakes" in this game. For temporarily I relinquish my claim to them and place them at the disposal of that *X* which might possibly turn out to be God.

What happens when I act like that?

Every experiment is a question put to the being from which I expect an answer. That answer may be affirmative if I have based my experiment on correct assumptions, or it may be negative if my assumptions were false and the experiment fails. But how will *God* react when I perform my experiment with him and agree to the bet?

If he is the one his witnesses confess him to be, he will speak up and let me know that it was no empty game or masquerade when I tentatively assumed the role of believer and acted "as if" he existed. Then he will let me become certain that by this means I have not entered a game, but have come into the truth. For by this experimental behavior "as if" he existed, including the necessity of putting my passions on the line, I have "sought him with all my heart." I have not tried to get him for nothing. My willingness to play for high stakes proved that I did not want to have my life to myself, hoping to keep God out of it. God "lets himself be found" (Jer. 29:13) by people like that, who put their lives on the line. Having done that, I have made the first move in the wager. Now it is God's turn. In the next moment I will see *if* he is and *who* he is.

That is the wager on God.

In the following chapters I wish to speak with people who, out of this readiness to put themselves on the line, are asking about God. The present preliminary conversation with the reader differs markedly in style and method of presentation from the chapters that follow. They contain addresses which I made in St Michael's Church in Hamburg. As usual, the congregations there were varied—a great many young people, but also the elderly; intellectuals and simple souls; professors and dock workers; captains of industry and humble clerks. More recently, as an extension of the worship service, several hundred listeners gathered for a lively discussion in which they wrestled with problems brought up by the sermon. On such occasions the question examined on the preceding pages came up again and again, for many—indeed most—of those present were not church-going people. They were seeking, straying, but also troubled. My work has been principally intended for them. Even though they asked a broad spectrum of very diverse questions, through them all ran the red thread of inquiry about God and about the possibility of greater certainty. In this opening word I wanted to let the reader in on the basic question, the one that so greatly occupied my listeners and dominated every discussion period.

Betting on God

If I now may put down in a few sentences what ties this introductory essay with the sermons that follow, I would say that my concern was to answer the question "And if there *be* a God . . . ?" by speaking about people to whom God became a certainty. Further, I wanted to interpret texts that were written in the name of this certainty. In other words, I wanted to indicate the level on which one's life moves when one brings God into the picture. I wanted to show what that "as if" that lets us experiment with God looks like. I wanted to reflect a glimmer of that new life in which we can believe again, hope again, and love again. I wanted to display the magnitude of the fulfillment we can count on if we let ourselves in on the experiment with God.

In general, I don't think much of book or lecture titles that promise some basis on which we can "still" be Christian. That sounds dreadfully resigned and backward-looking. It gives the impression of a rearguard action, defending deserted fortifications (like Spengler's "Soldier of Pompeii") and moving toward a "twilight of the Gods." The word "still" is notoriously unchristian, because it is without hope. In the New Testament the word "already" plays a much greater and radiant role: "Already" the axe is laid to the root of the trees (Matt. 3:10)—I came to cast fire on the earth, and would that it were "already" kindled (Luke 12:49). "Already" the fields are white for harvest (John 4:35). Not that I have "already" obtained this or am already perfect . . . that all lies ahead (Phil. 3:12, 13). Thus we live in the name of that which is promised to us and which, above all, is to come. Christians are people who live not from the pluperfect of "still" but from the future perfect "already."

In this book, therefore, I want to show what we let ourselves in for when we dare to reckon with God. I want to look at the second move in the game with God—the move in which God reveals himself as the master of the game.

But isn't all that only a poor analogy after all? Are we really the initiators of the game and God merely the reactor? Actually it is just another mental exercise which we write on the board only to erase again. For what does it really mean to say that

God is master of the game and that he reveals himself when it is his turn to move? Isn't he very much more than merely the master player? Isn't he already at work in me when I become ready to risk the game in the first place?

There is a whole cascade of discoveries which begin to pour forth in ever new streams when I sit down to bet on God.

PART ONE:

How to Believe Again

1. WHO IS A GOD-SEEKER?

Entering Jericho he [Jesus] made his way through the city. There was a man there named Zacchaeus; he was superintendent of taxes and very rich. He was eager to see what Jesus looked like; but, being a little man, he could not see him for the crowd. So he ran on ahead and climbed a sycamore tree in order to see him, for he was to pass that way. When Jesus came to the place, he looked up and said, "Zacchaeus, be quick and come down; I must come and stay with you today." He climbed down as fast as he could and welcomed him gladly. At this there was a general murmur of disapproval. "He has gone in," they said, "to be the guest of a sinner." But Zacchaeus stood there and said to the Lord, "Here and now, sir, I give half my possessions to charity; and if I have cheated anyone, I am ready to repay him four times over." Jesus said to him, "Salvation has come to this house today! —for this man too is a son of Abraham, and the Son of Man has come to seek and save what is lost."

Luke 19:1–10

In a literal sense, Jericho was an accursed spot. Back in the dim past, Joshua had cast a curse on this place, and the old histories reported strange and somewhat weird stories of how this condemnation was fulfilled.

As far as scenery was concerned, Jericho was almost as beautiful as the garden of Eden. It was noted for its palms; but it was also notorious for its snakes. Just as in the original Paradise, the heavenly and the hellish were closely interwoven.

The name of Jericho has a significant ring to us as Christians in another respect too. We know it from Jesus' parable about the priest and Levite who needlessly passed by the beaten man —they were on the way to Jericho. But the merciful Samaritan had Jericho as his goal too. This "little town" is like Thornton Wilder's *Our Town*—it is a world in miniature. It had cold clerics and pious men of God, exploiters and exploited. In many respects you could call it a miniature Hamburg or New York,

25

for Jericho also was, in its way, a "gateway to the world"—even though in pocket size. It was a transfer point for commerce. No wonder, then, that there were packs of tax officers, superintendents of taxes, and tax collectors. They were neither civil servants nor paid by government wage scales. They got a portion of their intake and also made a "rebate" for their own pocket. You need only take the affection shown for our own financial officials, scrupulous though they are, as a standard to imagine what friendly thoughts the people in Jericho entertained whenever they saw a tax collector on the street. On top of that, these gentlemen were also the agents of the Roman occupation forces. The common phrase, "tax collectors and sinners," reminds us even today of what untrustworthy rascals they were.

After thus setting the mood and looking at the background against which our drama will be played, I now come at last to the figure that stands at the center of the scenario: the superintendent of taxes and president of the Jericho board of finance, Zacchaeus. Actually he doesn't "stand" at the center of the scene, he is crouching in the limbs of a sycamore tree. Mr President was small in stature and it didn't do much good for him to stand on tip-toe. He needed to add yards to his height, so he joined the street urchins in the tree.

It is important to keep the comic side of this action in mind, so that its real meaning can be grasped. No one—especially not a president—relishes showing the world that he comes up a little short where size is concerned. He doesn't voluntarily put himself in situations that border on the ludicrous. People usually trembled before this bureau chief; seeing him sitting up in a tree certainly must have given the crowd a fiendish delight. But Zacchaeus takes it. His feverish excitement over the man from Nazareth is so great that he forgets his inhibitions.

Precisely that is the first thought the Evangelist conveys to us. Zacchaeus is a seeker, and he seeks with such passion that he forgets himself. Thoughts about the consequences of his act—the possible curse of ludicrousness, or the loss of reputation and authority—simply didn't occur to him. "Christianity" certainly wasn't a means to improve his position in society and wrap him in an aura of respectability. In this case "Christianity" put him in a compromising situation. Since he overlooked all this, we must assume that his inner man was totally captivated.

No one ever stands on ceremony during an emergency. After an air raid I once saw a prominent man who had leaped out of a burning house wearing one black boot and one brown shoe. It looked extremely funny. Yet when it's a matter of life and death things like that don't bother us. For Zacchaeus it is a matter of life and death. Therefore he sits up in the tree with the children.

Who or what was he seeking?

Quite simply, he was eager to see Jesus, to see "who he really was." Significantly, it does not say he was eager to become acquainted with what Jesus "did" or what he "said." He was concerned about the man himself; he was concerned with the heart of the matter, not the periphery. After all, this is a serious matter to Zacchaeus. So he must get to the heart of this problem called "Jesus of Nazareth."

This point is true of all of us. Granted, there are many words handed down from this Nazarene that touch us deeply: the parable of the prodigal son, for example, or the words about God's care for the lilies of the field. But we can read similar things in the Bhagavadgita. Furthermore, there is hardly a word Jesus said, at least as far as form is concerned, that can't be read in previous rabbinical literature. The words of Jesus, taken by themselves, can never be my sole support in life and death. On the contrary, they can never free me from the doubt that my salvation lies with someone else, that I ought to seek it through Buddha, or Zarathustra, or Gandhi. These, too, have spoken great words, words that get under your skin. In that respect, Jesus of Nazareth is just one among many. What he said and did—and certainly that was a great deal—still would not be enough for one to be able to live by, unless he himself was who he was.

The whole story of the prodigal son—what good does it do me without him, without his being who he is? Without him it is a touching tale about a father who doesn't give up his erring son, and who finally receives him back into his waiting arms. Naturally that is a beautiful story. I would even say that it is a masterpiece of unmatched form and content. And quite naturally it touches me. But—and this is the real question —how do I get to the point where I can believe that the father in this story is God himself and that this God deals with me exactly the way the father did in the parable: That he lets me fall, even though I am as I am, and that he finally receives me with honor? *That* is the point of this story! If I don't come to that point, if I can't "apply" it to myself, then this story is just good writing, nothing more.

There is only one condition under which it becomes clear to me that it is really God *himself* who presents himself to me as father and that I am not falling prey to empty rhetoric. That condition is that I am convinced by him who knows all this and who reports and proclaims it on his own personal responsibility. If this man's actions become transparent and the figure of the Father with his open arms appears through them; if Paul's words about him—that he is "the image of the invisible God"—are correct; and if Luther is right in designating him as a mirror of God's fatherly heart; then, only then, can I accept what he has to say. Then, and only then, can he be the guarantee of my faith.

Therefore, we seek no dogma and no teaching; we seek the figure of the Lord himself. Teaching and dogma may harbor profound thoughts. Their deep meaning, storing up the spiritual experience of centuries, may fascinate us intellectually. But in the final analysis all that would be trash and religious nonsense if the belief-inspiring figure of Jesus himself did not stand behind it. If it was not *he* from whom we accepted it and in whom we could believe, then both he and the teaching would be nothing but "poetic license." With the hyperalert instinct of a man who knows he has reached the moment of truth in his life, Zacchaeus tracks down the crucial question: This man who is passing by, who sticks with the blind and the lame and never is too grown up for a child, who radiates power and love—this man must convince him, this man must be believable, otherwise everything he has heard from him and about him is sheer hokum.

It pays to climb a tree and to do the unusual if that's the only way to become certain about this decisive entry in the ledger of your life.

Whoever seeks in that heedless way must be ever dissatisfied with himself. Certainly Zacchaeus had far more to worry about than his small size. When Jesus has brought him down from his tree and Zacchaeus looks up into his face, the dam breaks. All those untamed elements in his life pour out: "Believe me: I'm turning over half of everything I have to the poor, and if I have squeezed anyone (that is the literal reading of the original), I will replace it four times over."

At first it could almost appear that Zacchaeus was just uttering pious moral platitudes or even that he wanted to brag a little: "Isn't that right, Jesus of Nazareth? To give ten percent of one's income is considered very fine, but look, *I'm* giving fifty! And if I have swindled anyone, then I'll do four hundred percent worth of penance."

However, any careful observer would not have to be a psychology major to perceive that Zacchaeus does none of these things for his own prestige; he simply wants to confess. He acknowledges that he has come to a dead end. The moral experiment which he attempted in all seriousness doesn't work. In that experiment he tried (admittedly in a somewhat extreme fashion and with a little extortion thrown in) what all of us have tried, even though we may not go as far or get in as deep.

One of us may have pulled a somewhat crooked deal in filling out his tax return, and as a tranquilizer for his conscience he writes a cheque for that amount to charity. Another has transformed a business trip into a little rendezvous and when his conscience begins to bother him on the way home he digs deep into his pocket and buys a pearl necklace for his wife, who breaks into tears at the thoughtfulness of her devoted husband. Still another is a businessman who prides himself on being a man of action. He has no qualms about walking right over people when it seems expedient to do so. To avoid the pangs of a bad conscience, he seeks to justify himself by some public beneficence. Perhaps he buys some organ pipes or a stained glass window for the church, so that everyone who hears of it is very impressed with such an excess of selflessness.

Zacchaeus, however, is not impressed by his own selflessness, even when he repays damages by four hundred percent. He knows only too well what his trouble is: His whole life is one continuous battle against a bad conscience. At night he is pursued by visions of people he has wronged or put in a tight spot. At home his chandelier and his carpet ask him who their rightful owners really are. They want to know if he thinks it proper that the one stays in the dark and the other in the light. And it is remarkable that the radiant and thankful faces of those he has made happy by his voluntary contributions cannot banish the ghostly appearances of those he has hurt.

No one has any idea what a battlefield of conflicting thoughts Zacchaeus's soul has become. Some people honor him because he has been generous to them, and others hate him because he has exploited them. But no one sees the internal schism in which he has involved himself. He is so alone that he never once compares himself to others, saying perhaps "the rest of the boys are worse than I am; they squeeze just as I do, but they don't have the misgivings I have. So they don't try to make it up."

Zacchaeus is so saddled with the unsolved question of guilt in his life that what other men do is of no concern to him. He not only couldn't care less whether they saw him in his ridiculous situation in the sycamore tree, but he even neglects to cast a self-satisfied glance at how much more evil other men's practices are than his own.

Once we understand what is out of order in our lives, then we stand alone before God—all alone. For guilt always isolates. Zacchaeus knows that he will not be able to get out of this dark corridor by himself—that someone from outside must bring a light and come and get him. Therefore he looks with burning gaze on the Man who is passing by, asking himself if he holds the power that will release him from the captivity of his life.

Really, Zacchaeus is all eyes and ears as he tries to establish who this Jesus of Nazareth might be. Therefore he is truly a seeker. He desires nothing less than the loosing of his chains.

There is also another type—the pseudoseekers. They pride themselves on being struggling men, wandering like Faust between two worlds. But basically they don't want to find anything. Because when we find God we are immediately taken into his service, placed on the track of our neighbor, and faced with an absolute demand. The pseudoseekers, however, don't want that. They only want the romance of being on the way; they are enamored of the pressing on, the "eternal striving effort" that Goethe prizes, because that obligates them to nothing. One can even take that need (that rootless, goalless, uncertainty) and make a virtue out of it; it can become a sort of Faustian flirtation with fate. All of that is make-believe; it brings no blessing. Zacchaeus, however, is a man who seeks so hard that he doesn't even realize he is a "seeker." He is gripped by the solution to his life's question, coming toward him now in the form of this one Man.

Then comes Zacchaeus's first surprise.

He wanted to observe this phenomenon called Jesus of Nazareth from the perspective of a spectator. He wanted to let him pass in review, so to speak, so that he could form an opinion. But it didn't happen the way he had expected. His role as spectator is suddenly ended. For Jesus stops, looks at him, and calls him by his name: "Zacchaeus, come down as quickly as you can, tonight I am to be a guest in your house." That is the first great miracle—that Jesus *knows* him. Zacchaeus, the seeker, is on the way to find Jesus, wondering if this man will have the liberating word he needs, and if this Nazarene is trustworthy. And meanwhile the one sought is already on the way to *him*. In the drama of his life, where he seemed to be standing on the stage all alone, carrying on a despairing monologue, another voice joins the play. This other has already been on his trail for a long time. Can we make Zacchaeus's revolutionary discovery in our own lives? It is the same discovery, made in a new way, when we learn that our search ultimately involves a *person* rather than "the" truth—that it is not a doctrine of salvation that brings newness into our lives, but that it is the Savior himself, a living being.

The great eye expert, Jung-Stilling, whose childlike piety made him beloved even by Goethe, once received a deeply touching letter from Immanuel Kant. In that letter the great thinker included the sentence, "My dear Dr Jung, I am quite certain that you do well to seek your only consolation in the Gospel, for it is the inexhaustible source of all truths which, after Reason has surveyed its whole field, can be found nowhere else." When that is written by a man like Kant, who devoted his whole life to an unrelenting self-criticism of thought, it naturally makes an impression on us. Far be it from me to find fault with it. And yet Kant has missed the real secret of the Gospel because he describes the greatness of this Gospel as follows: After Reason has surveyed its whole field, it must pull up in amazement before this Gospel, because here things are learned and spoken which surpass all human knowledge and which even the greatest power of thought cannot master—these things therefore must come as gifts. The Gospel is revelation of the ultimate secret of life; it is gracefully guaranteed knowledge. That is what Kant sees in the Gospel.

But is that really correct? Do we actually have to start by measuring out the whole field of Reason before we can come to the Gospel? If that is the case, what shall the ten lepers do, or those who are mentally disturbed and in the state hospital? What will the sick black man in Lambarene do when the field of Reason remains closed to him? And what shall we ourselves do, if a frightful illness gets a stranglehold on us, if a crazy problem won't let us sleep, or if someone cheats us? Maybe we are meditative people through and through, who take the question of truth seriously. Perhaps we ponder the meaning of our life. Yet we all are well enough aware that there are "pressure tests," boundary situations in our life, where all that becomes pointless, where the blood drains from our brain, our nerves are on fire, and just one more pain, one more anxiety, or one more passion will shatter us. If it were simply a matter of knowledge about God and if the Gospel were just a teaching about this knowledge, then none of it would help us at all. When Peter was sinking in the waves, he didn't call out, "Lord, teach me how to get out of this!" He cried, "Lord, help me!" And the centurion from Capernaum, whose servant was writhing in torment, didn't say, "Jesus of Nazareth, enlighten me medically about what should be done, or—in case nothing more can be done—tell me something about the meaning of suffering in the world, so that I may at least be able to cope with it spiritually." No indeed, he said, "Lord, speak only a word and my servant will be healed."

They all seek something other than a *teaching* about guilt and sorrow and the problems of life. They seek the Savior who forgives the guilt and takes away the sorrow. They search for him who does not merely *solve* the problems intellectually, but who *resolves* the inner conflicts that those problems create.

Certainly there are great and profound teachings in the world. But one must have the capacity to understand them, and one must be in a situation which affords the reason adequate breathing space. The greatness of the Gospel lies in the fact that it is available to *all*: not only to the spiritually mature or great, such as Kant, but also to the weak. Pascal with his sublimest intellectual world of thought can find it, but so can a little girl who prays each night as she goes to bed, "Now I lay me down to sleep, I pray the Lord my soul to keep."

Both the New Testament and the hymns of the church indicate that all of us (even we who are mature, rational, and intellectually polished to a high sheen) know moments when we are a heap of misery, no longer able to speak in orderly, meaningful sentences, but only able to "sigh" (Rom. 8:26). Those who look for salvation from a teaching or even from a Christian theological dogma, are betrayed and cheated when, perhaps reduced to a bundle of nerves, they can only sigh. For sighing and knowing, groaning and thinking, are two different things.

Those, however, who know that they have to do with a living heart, a Savior, and not with the "it" of dogma or of profound knowledge are certain of one thing (and that is so amazing that no one can comprehend it). They are certain that even their last sigh, the fragments of sentences and scraps of words from the dying and even the mentally ill reach that heart, that they are still heard and understood in love. "Though I may not feel thy might," as the hymn says, though I may not find it in my thoughts any more, though I can no longer see, taste, and feel, "it guides me even through the night."

Sometimes during the last war my students wrote me from the battlefield, and one sentence came up again and again in countless variations: "I am so exhausted from marching, my stomach is so empty, I am so plagued with lice and scratching, I am so tormented by the biting cold of Russia and so dead tired, that I am totally occupied, without the least bit of inner space for any speculative thinking. I haven't only forgotten Hölderlin and the other authors I read in school, I'm even too weak to leaf through the Bible. I am even lazy about the Lord's Prayer. My whole spiritual life is disorganized and ruined. I just vegetate."

How should I answer these young men? I wrote them, "Be thankful that the Gospel is more than a philosophy. If it were only a philosophy, you would just have it as long as you could keep it in mind and it could afford you intellectual comfort. But even when you can no longer think about God, he still thinks about you."

Precisely *that* is the miracle of the Gospel. We are not the only ones on the way. There is another coming to meet us who knows us. If we can feel nothing of his presence, he still feels for us. If we sit in a leafy observation post like Zacchaeus, reviewing what various religions and philosophies have to offer us, and weighing whether it might pay to give Jesus of Nazareth a closer look in the contest, he has already seen us. He knows our name and calls out to us, "Come down quickly, I'm coming to see you." All that lies in the fact that we are dealing with a living Savior rather than with an idea of salvation or with Christian ethics. And while we are seeking the heart of all things, a home is being prepared for us in that heart. We, however, never dream it could be happening.

Zacchaeus found that out. For he was concerned about Jesus as a person; he wanted to find out who he really was. Now he knows. Now his future has begun. The moment can be fixed

34

precisely: "Today" salvation has come to this house. Wherever contact with Jesus Christ occurs, there salvation has come.

The people who watched this scene in and under the sycamore tree probably set up an angry clamor, including some boos. For the Nazarene passed by the elite who stood at the doors of their villas, he passed by the higher and lower clergy who helped form a cordon to keep back the crowd; then he brought this shady half-pint down out of his tree. Furthermore, he was going to visit Zacchaeus's home, where he would recline on a carpet—and everyone knew how the gentleman from the tax office had come by his luxurious furniture. The people probably did not voice their discontent with Zacchaeus himself (since they were not especially well informed about him). What mattered was the mere fact that he was "one of them," one of the suspected group of tax collectors. Wasn't Jesus of Nazareth aware that he would compromise himself when he broke the taboo by setting foot in the outlaw's house?

The reaction of the crowd is a human one—all too human.

We are only too inclined to collective condemnations of that sort. Zacchaeus the individual may be what he will; he may do more good than evil. But he has already been thrown into a moral pigeon hole, simply because his occupation classes him with the bloodsuckers.

And this is the second miracle that Zacchaeus encounters.

Jesus Christ never puts us in pigeon holes. In his eyes every man, in and for himself, is a child of his heavenly Father, whom he seeks and for whom he suffers. That is true once and for all. The assistant executioners who held their macabre games of dice and their drinking bouts at the foot of the cross were not crossed off his list because they belonged to the class called "enemies." Even in death he maintains an individual interest in each of those rude roughnecks, and his last thoughts seek to keep their souls from jeopardy. "Father, forgive them, for they know not what they do." And even though he knew that the rich young man would get up the next moment and leave in exasperation, perhaps to join the opposition or the bored army of the indifferent, Jesus looked at him and loved him and welcomed him. It was that love which he not only taught but

35

which he lived; the love that never identified a man with the class in which he fell, but always considered the man to be more than what he did. Even in the most questionable rascal, he still saw his Father's prodigal son, over whom the Father grieved.

Therefore, one cannot generate this love by means of morality. Maybe my landlady is an ugly witch, my boss a monster, or my colleague a perfect example of mediocrity who sends me up the wall every day. If I were to tell myself, "Despite everything, you must 'love' these splendid specimens (as it says in the Bible)," the result would be nothing but a frightful sham. My attempt to spread a smile of greeting across my face would only end in a grimace. We all have encountered these pseudo-Christian grimaces of an artificial friendliness, and we have realized that they were pure sham.

So that doesn't work. But one can reach a point in Jesus' school where he can see a quite different side to his irritating neighbors. He recognizes them as living souls whom God has destined for his own—living souls for whom he suffers and who suffer themselves. It is a dazzling revelation to discover all at once that there is good reason to pity someone whom you have previously considered worthy only of contempt. You have a passionate desire to help and to free him from his prison. You are suddenly "for" someone else. For love in Jesus' sense of the word is no sentimental feeling; it means nothing less than to be there for the other person, to discover in him something new and revolutionary.

And yet as far as Jesus is concerned there is more involved than just the individual and his own soul. He does not say "today salvation has come to you" but ". . . to your house." Since you, Zacchaeus, have this day been brought into the sunshine out of the dark house of your life, there is no way you can avoid reflecting and reradiating the light-rays from eternity that have struck you. When Jesus steps into a life, he starts a chain reaction that goes on and on. My household notices something of it, and so do my surroundings. For everything is completely different. Our eyes are renewed, and suddenly we have a completely different picture of our neighbor from what we had before. The same force that overturned our life and set us on a new course will not let us rest until we have passed on the message of what brought us joy and gave us peace. He who stands in the light must, in turn, radiate that light. As Moses came down from Sinai, he had to veil his face, because the encounter with God had left his face glowing with an intolerable brilliance.

No one leaves the encounter with Jesus Christ the same as when he came. For Jesus is the great transformer. A teacher of wisdom can't manage that, because his goal is to make himself superfluous. A student has no thanks for a teacher who never lets him graduate. But with Jesus Christ we go from one transformation to another. He gives us the brightness of morning as the day begins. He wraps us in his peace when the typewriters clatter and the telephone rings all day long. And in the evening I can let myself drop, because his hand is always beneath me.

He gives me joy in life and companionship in my final distress. And when I must stand in the final judgment, he will intercede for me because he has endured pain to draw me to himself and make me his own. The man from Nazareth stands between me and every shadow, for he has called me by my name, he has brought me down from my airy spectator's seat in the tree, and now there is nothing else in the world that can come between me and the final fulfillment of my life.

2. THE POINT ON WHICH I STAND
OR FALL

When he came to the territory of Caesarea Philippi, Jesus asked his disciples, "Who do men say that the Son of Man is?" They answered, "Some say John the Baptist, others Elijah, others Jeremiah, or one of the prophets." "And you," he asked, "who do you say I am?" Simon Peter answered: "You are the Messiah, the Son of the living God." Then Jesus said: "Simon son of Jonah, you are favoured indeed! You did not learn that from mortal man; it was revealed to you by my heavenly Father. And I say this to you: You are Peter, the Rock; and on this rock I will build my church, and the powers of death shall never conquer it. I will give you the keys of the kingdom of Heaven; what you forbid on earth shall be forbidden in heaven, and what you allow on earth shall be allowed in heaven." He then gave his disciples strict orders not to tell anyone that he was the Messiah.

From that time Jesus began to make it clear to his disciples that he had to go to Jerusalem, and there to suffer much from the elders, chief priests, and doctors of the law; to be put to death and to be raised again on the third day. At this Peter took him by the arm and began to rebuke him: "Heaven forbid!" he said. "No, Lord, this shall never happen to you." Then Jesus turned and said to Peter, "Away with you, Satan; you are a stumbling-block to me. You think as men think, not as God thinks."

Matthew 16:13–23

Mars doesn't care whether we believe it is inhabited or an icy wilderness. But Jesus cares what we think about him. He is deeply concerned about whether and how well we get along with him. And all of us ask about him as well. This question takes many forms.

It can be the question of the intellectually curious, who would like to learn about the historical circumstances surrounding that remarkable figure who struck the first spark of this complex, enigmatic and unquenchable phenomenon called Christianity. On the other hand, the question about Christ can be put very personally: Did the secret of life really come to light in this man? Does it therefore follow that the secret and meaning of my own life does not lie in some universal formula which I must ferret out, but in the love which this man from Nazareth displayed in his life—a life lived without regard for the cost? That would mean that I would not become angry with anyone —never under any circumstances—simply because that person counts for something with my heavenly Father and has a place in his heart.

We all ask about him. Even the cool calculator who thinks only of results knows moments when he sneaks a furtive glance at the crucifix, barely breathing the question, "Was that Nazarene right after all?" Might it really be no profit to me to have won the whole world, piled up money and influence, and perhaps become famous, when all the time I was actually bringing harm to my soul? Might I have missed the mark and set my life on the wrong track when I passed by this one man from Nazareth at the very moment when the good lay so close at hand?

But no matter how we ask about him—be it openly or secretly, ardently or despairingly—one thing is sure, he is also asking about us. He is edging his way through the crowd toward me and toward you, intent in every fiber of his being upon letting us find him.

Our text shows how moving it is for him to hear any sort of responsive echo from a human heart or to see the first light of understanding dawn when people realize who it is they have before them. "What do people actually say about me, the Son of Man? Who am I in their eyes?" With this inquiry our text gets under way.

It is important to fix precisely the point in Jesus' life at which he posed this question. He asks it at the apex of his life, shortly before its curve turns steeply downward, heading for the great debacle—from a human point of view—and the final end in the death cry of one forsaken by God. But at this point he *still* stands at the zenith of his career, the masses *still* occupy him, and he creates a sensation wherever he appears. The eyewitnesses of his great moments can still be interviewed personally. One can talk with people and see for oneself the former

39

cripple who now can walk again or the mental case who has had the burden lifted from his soul.

Of course, the forces of opposition are already stirred up too. A subterranean rumble becomes audible in this life, which leads one to conclude that, in the field of force surrounding Jesus the conquering power of the kingdom of God is not the only force at work. The opponents, the demonic powers, are also active.

Even at a distance the double secret of this life begins to reveal itself. On the one hand a trail of victory follows on his heels, a trail that leads into your life and my life today. Here one comes into peace with God and finds the meaning of his life again. Here the chains of our bondage are broken and the fear of death is removed. Here an eternal hand lies in our own.

But another secret also begins to come to light. The figure of the *Savior*, of all things, leaves a trail of blood behind. Terror, clericalism and intolerance dog his heels. There is no horror of any sort of inquisition, no witch trial, no stake, no diabolical trick that will not also be perpetrated in its name—the name of a so-called Christianity.

It is apparent that wherever the Savior shows up everything, including the opposition, is aroused and swings into action. He awakens homesickness for the father's house in the prodigal son, but hate and obduracy spring up in the elder brother. Depraved souls are brought back into line, but the demons rise up and tug at their chains.

Everything between heaven and hell, eternal and abysmal, becomes "virulent" and swings into action where he appears. Above him sing the angels, and beneath him murmurs the deep. Nothing remains unmoved when he appears, and nothing remains unchanged after having encountered him. The waves become still at his command, and the earth quakes when he cries out in death. Animated hearts and inanimate elements start vibrating. There are men who find peace through him; but Judas, too, goes to work.

This man is truly a problem; he seems to shimmer in all colors. He can't be reduced to a formula. *Who might he be?* What is going on here?

40

"What do the people actually say about me? Who do you think I am?" he himself asks. He receives quite respectable answers to these questions. The people reach for nothing but superlatives to describe the impression he has made on them. They call him the reincarnation of the greatest figures in their history: "Jeremiah, Elijah, or one of the prophets." That is their way of saying that he belongs in the skyline of that massive range which displays the high points of God's guidance and mighty acts in their history. In order to put the appearance of Jesus into words, the people have to cite the almost mythical figures of their past.

We must be clear about what it means for the people to place a living man, known to all, in such larger-than-life and practically legendary company. That happens more easily after a man has been dead for a while. For time retouches and gilds the images in our memory. But, as I said before, here it is a living man (with a home address!) who is being placed in the "Hall of Fame."

Yet this respectable certificate of character issued to him by the public may have caused Jesus great sorrow. "Certainly," he may have said to himself, "they consider you to be very prominent, and that occupies their imagination to an unusual degree. But they simply have no concept of the focus of your life or of its decisive direction. To be sure, they consider you to be a prophet, that is, they think you know more about divine mysteries than ordinary people do. They think you are someone through whom God's majesty shines more purely and more clearly, someone in whom he is more accurately 'represented' than in other men. But that also means that they consider you to be only the highest *human* possibility that they can imagine.

"For them," he may think, "I am simply someone who stands on this side of the great gulf of guilt and death, the gulf between time and eternity. For them I am the highest-reaching human hand, the hand which is permitted to stretch farthest across that gulf until it feels the touch of the Father's hand. But they do not see me as the outstretched hand of the Father *himself*. And yet it is precisely that that makes the difference. That is what I wish to bring them. No one else on earth can convey to them what I do. I come from the other side; I am that fatherly hand itself, the good hand which places itself on the wounds of my human brothers, which comforts them as a mother comforts them, and which slips beneath their head at death to lead them dreaming to the other side. In their touching love and their tendency to applaud me they never once have caught a glimpse of all that."

He is very lonely at this moment, and the praise of men (including their "Christian standpoint") is merely a misunderstanding which does not do him justice—exactly as the Christianity of later generations will only too often be just another name for the misunderstandings which have formed around Jesus of Nazareth.

In that event it may have been even more crucial for him to know whether his friends and followers were in on a little *more* of his secret. After all, they knew him best; as his companions they had shared in his everyday life. "Then who do *you* say that I am?"

Our text reaches its climax in the words that now are spoken.

For Peter feels himself driven to a confession the madness of which (there's no other way to put it) hardly hits us any more because, in the meantime, the words have become all too familiar. They have long since become a Christian cliché. But at the time this confession was uttered, it must have been a powerful shock to those who heard it.

Peter says, "You are the Messiah, the Son of the living God." That is to say, "You are not one of us. You are not even a polished special edition of the species man; you are totally different." "You are the Messiah." That means, "We men stand on the lowest step; we wave from afar; we build dream castles and move farther from the goal. But *you* come from the Father's lighted house while we sneak around hopelessly outside. You come to meet us from the other side. At best, perhaps, we are people who must toil 'upward still and onward,'[1] yet never knowing how the adventure of our life will end. But you

1. James Russell Lowell, "Once to every man and nation."

come from the fulfillment. We sing 'Peace is there that knows no measure,'[2] but you come from that peace, you *are* peace itself."

When Jesus broke the silence that followed this precedent-shattering statement (and there must have been a pause of astonishment and confusion) he explained to Peter and the onlookers that this statement itself was a miracle. It was miraculous that such words could be uttered at all. "Flesh and blood," mere instinct or mother-wit, could not have discovered this secret. For one moment the walls of fog that mysteriously shroud the figure of Jesus of Nazareth are parted, and the eyes of an incomprehensible majesty gaze upon a stunned Peter.

At that moment Peter is the loneliest man on the face of the earth. He is almost as lonely as the Master himself. Formerly Peter was a man like everybody else. He was a man like you and me. He affirmed God's providence when things suited him, and he protested when they got in his way. He wanted to do the right thing, but consciousness of his sin weighed on him like a millstone. He had not settled matters with his own conscience and therefore, with good reason, steered clear of the circuit of the eternal Judge.

That's the way it usually is with all of us. Peter was no different from you and me. But now, at one blow, all that changes. Now he is the only one who has felt the scales drop from his eyes. Now he sees that God's heartbeat can be touched and felt and heard, despite all of life's riddles, all the world's horrors, and even judgment itself. *You* are the assurance (Peter is now able to confess) that there is no "Fate," but that, far above our heads, there are higher and loving thoughts about us. *You* are the assurance that there is something other than the eternal law of crime and punishment, that there is a Father who forgives our incriminating past and gives us the miracle of a fresh start.

In the strict sense of the word, Peter's discovery is a miracle. Neither a sensitivity for metaphysical questions nor a genius for religion could have enabled him to penetrate that wall of

2. John Bowring, "In the Cross of Christ I glory."

fog. Such traits are merely the power of "flesh and blood," they remain captive to human limitations.

Jesus responds to this event by conferring on Peter a sort of title as the "Exception." He expresses the uniqueness of this breakthrough in the form of a privilege which he bestows on him. "You are Peter, the Rock: and on this Peter-Rock I will build my church, so that the gates of the underworld cannot overpower it." In this way Jesus intends to imply that the church will live at all times by doing what Peter did in this moment. It must be able to see *God himself* behind the figure of the carpenter's son from Nazareth. Behind the casual figure of this one man who is virtually lost in the vast panorama of history, the church must discern the God who stretches his hand over the globe, over East and West, over the public summit conference of the mighty and the secret rendezvous of lovers, over electronic brains and sparrows, over rockets and roses, over our first parents in Paradise and over men at the end of the world.

How can the church really be built on a rock like that, a rock so firm that she will not be blown over by the storm of hostile ideologies nor undercut by the rotten tide of our affluence? It depends exclusively on her constant reliving of that one moment that was the miracle of Caesarea Philippi, so that she discovers the lordship of Jesus and never wavers, even when Golgotha comes and heaven seems to look the other way.

Yet we cannot step lightly over the broad expanse of these words "You are Peter . . ." which are written in mighty letters around the cupola of St Peter's and which have become the shibboleth of our Catholic-Protestant division. We cannot rush on to the dramatic twist at the end of the story. For this conversation does not have a happy ending. It leads to a totally unexpected catastrophe. The man who had just been praised as a "Rock of God" and held up as the bearer of much promise is in the next moment decried as a "Satan" consigned to the enemy camp. And I dare say that the drama between Christ and all of us is presented in the tension between those two poles of our text. It is compressed in the two lapidary phrases of Jesus, "You are Peter" and "You are a Satan."

What's up here? Jesus has considered it proper to prepare his disciples carefully for the fact that he, the Son of the living God, is about to enter upon the path of suffering and loneliness. The crowds will melt away, and his life must end in the forsakenness of the night on Golgotha. Men will talk about everything—the political situation, production, the developing nations, surcharges and tariffs, the atomic boom—about everything but him. He will be surrounded by a great silence. But Peter doesn't stand for that. He is bewildered by the downward turn in Jesus' career; he balks at it, seizing Jesus by the arm and protesting in words that could either stem from the need for self-assurance or from a faith that hopes against hope: "Nothing like that could ever happen to you; that is simply impossible!"

Why does Peter shrink back from that path of suffering? Is he worried, perhaps, that he will have to share this path of pain? That is certainly *not* the explanation of his protest, for we have no reason to assume that Peter was lacking in physical courage. His protest really arises from the apparent utter senselessness of it all. Why should the One who exceeds all human powers be trampled underfoot by men? Why should he who has been allotted the farthest reaches of heaven be dragged through the deepest mud of earth?

If he really *was* the Christ, argued Peter, then he couldn't possibly end up in the weakness of death. And in saying that, Peter speaks for all mankind.

If he really *was* the Christ, then how could Christianity possibly be in the shape that it appears to be in, unfortunately, after two thousand years? How can he possibly remain quiet while thousands meet a horrible, silent fate without judge or justice under dictatorships or tyrannies, whether in Vietnam, Biafra, or anywhere else? Helpless and silent they go to their doom, and no cock crows afterward and no Christ intervenes. How can he possibly remain quiet about the horrors that are concealed in the "no visitors" sections of mental hospitals? How can he possibly remain quiet in the face of cancer and crippled children, multiple sclerosis and the tragedies of old age? How can he be silent instead of stepping in? But how shall

45

he be able to step in, how shall he act like a Savior, when he himself is crushed and ends up helpless on the scaffold? How indeed! "Nothing like this shall ever happen to you," cries out Peter—and so do we. It would be the bitterest end of the Christian dream if he was destined to end up as helpless as that.

This quibbling by his disciple gives Jesus a very anxious moment, because it instantly becomes clear that Peter hadn't the foggiest notion of what he had really said in his confession. "You are the Messiah, the Son of the living God." He had meant a Christ without suffering, and therefore he had not meant Christ at all. He wasn't at all clear on what he had said. The words so mysteriously given to him went right over his head.

Granted that when Peter made his statement he had recognized more in Jesus of Nazareth than the others had. He had seen that Jesus was different from all others who walked the earth. To mention only a few traits by which Peter might have detected this unique character of Jesus: He saw a love in him that broke through the world's law of retribution. He saw that he did not simply echo his hate-filled environment, but that he blessed those who cursed him. He saw that he did not abandon others when they renounced him. That was above and beyond what one experienced elsewhere in life. That was "unheard of."

And Peter saw even more. He saw how Jesus lived in perpetual dialogue with his Father. There, too, he differed from us. For when we men want to pray, we must first try to free ourselves from everything that would clutch our hearts to earth. We must "collect" ourselves and concentrate on God. But Jesus was different. He *came* from constant association with the Father, he didn't need to "prepare" himself; this association was the native environment from which he came. Prayer enables us to view from a great distance, so to speak, the place from which he comes in every moment. *That was what was different about him.* Peter had discovered this, and much else, about him; therefore he had lifted Jesus above all other men and given him a place by himself with the confession, "You are the Messiah, the Son of the living God."

46

What he had *not* understood was the decisive point, however, and in fact it was precisely at that decisive point that he went wrong. He began to quarrel with the necessity for this One and Only to suffer and to have a fate allotted to him that contradicted most painfully and senselessly both his rank and his mission.

Why had he not grasped this decisive point about Jesus?

Peter envisioned his master as the revolutionizer of the world. He would give the wheel of history a new turn and make the world a place of righteousness and peace. For him Jesus was a symbol of those utopias that are dreamed of in every age, from the thousand years' Reich to the classless society. "How else," thought Peter, "shall the love of God make itself known than by helping the deprived and violated obtain their rights, making wars to cease, and driving death from the world?"

But if this so-called savior does *not* do away with all that, if the world goes on at its same old pace in the same old way, if God becomes an object of scorn and that One who is the "mirror of the fatherly heart" is smashed by a howling bunch of soldiers, where in all that can the love of God be discerned? How can God make himself believable then? Isn't the irony of it enough to make you weep—that precisely the One who was to cure the world's misery is seized by that misery and dragged to the scaffold of weakness? "Where is God," thinks Peter, "when that is Christ's situation and things go the way they do?" He may think of that "idiot God" described by Wolfgang Borchert in his play *Outside the Door*—that poor old man, seized with compassion for mankind, but much too weak, senile, and dottering to be of any real help.

Peter has not yet grasped the deepest secret of God's love. For this love does not consist in God's making this world into a paradise. Indeed, the exact opposite is true. God must constantly give man up to his own hopelessness, his own pride, and his own failure.

Has not the German catastrophe shown us that, once we began to drink from the cup of ecstasy we had to drain it to the dregs, and that it took the sermons of the death and ruins all about us to burst our wanton bubble? And today doesn't it sometimes send a chill down our spines to realize that God could once again descend as our avenger upon our relentless dance around the golden calf, smashing our television sets and refrigerators, because our fascination with the baubles of comfort make us forget the need of our neighbor and the despair of our brothers who groan under oppression or waste away in nations plagued by famine? Isn't precisely this involved in the hard love of God, that he must use pain, his pain and ours, to bring us back to our senses? In fact, it would be less than genuine love if it prevented guilt from being punished on earth. If that happened men would forget entirely what guilt was all about.

That is exactly the point where God shows his love, for he *stays with* mankind in the witches' cauldron of our misery. His Son is with us in this cauldron; therefore we learn to know that, even in the judgment he imposes, the Father still holds his child by the hand. We hear his fatherly word, "Your pain is my pain, and my own heart cries out over your sentence and your punishment."

Every father feels twice the pain that he inflicts on his child when he punishes him. Therein lies the uniqueness of parental punishment—that in the final analysis every father and every mother are putting themselves under punishment too. And if we focus on the pedagogical side of the matter for a moment, we discover that it is not so much the physical pain of the spanking or the disgrace of the scolding that exerts an educational influence as it is the child's seeing that it grieves the father himself to do it. He thinks, "It grieves him because he loves me; he bears the punishment with me." If this pain of love is not felt, then the suspicion arises that the discipline is being administered out of terror instead of affection.

We find all of that in the suffering of Jesus: here God himself suffers with us, standing under his own judgment; here he himself grieves over the punishment he must bring upon us. Jesus Christ suffers all loneliness, all enmity, all forsakenness by God, all fear of death; he shares in the suffering of all temptations and all divine judgment upon human self-destruc-

48

tion. *That* is the love of God, you foolish Peter, *that* is the way it is! It does not escort us to earth from beyond the blue with heavenly sympathy and divine goodwill (what incurable optimists proceed to call "Providence"); it waits for us. Indeed, it waits for us in such a way that it walks beside us, suffering *with* us whatever judgment or terror we must endure, going through it as a brother at our side. Here, in the midst of our sorrow and anxiety, we grip the hand that will be scorched along with ours—here and nowhere else. God does not renounce his faithfulness to us. And while one hand must smite us, the other helps, holds, and comforts us.

Peter has farther to go before he can understand all that. This we have seen—and it took some effort to grasp it—how a crisis of belief arose for Peter and why Jesus would utter the shocking reprimand, "Away with you, Satan. Get out! You are a stumbling-block to me!" Peter had very definite ideas and opinions about what Christ must be and do, but they were human, all too human, ideas and opinions. And when things went otherwise as, for example, when he was called upon to walk the path of suffering and weakness instead of the envisioned road of world revolution, Peter dropped out. He wasn't interested anymore. And when he said, "No," his faith fell apart.

Here a part of the whole mystery of faith comes to light. He who suffers in silence and trust when God does not speak, even though, humanly speaking, he ought to; he who suffers in silence and trust when God suffers, instead of banging his fist on the world's table; he who suffers in silence and trust as God lets his sun rise on the evil and good instead of being a visible avenger to the evil and a similarly tangible protector to the good; he who endures all these enigmas, content through storm and night and horror to grip that one hand called Jesus Christ; he who dares to believe that this hand is linked to thoughts that move far above all enigmas of life and that at the same time it possesses power to bring storms and waves to a sudden and complete halt—he will be the first to gauge completely what it means to say, "You are Christ, the Son of the living God; you are the hand of the Father, you are the hand that suffers with me and trembles with me, remaining always and in all things faithful to me."

But *if* he begins to gauge this, he will also be overcome with an intimation of who he himself is, an intimation both fearful and comforting. And perhaps he will frame this discovery of his own abyss in words that are also from Peter, "Lord, depart from me, for I am a sinful man." I am not worthy to be brought into your presence and into your peace. I can hardly bear the thought that you would consider me worthy of your love.

The moment he says that, however, he will experience a miracle. For the Lord will *not* leave and will *not* turn away; he will say, "Precisely because you confess that you are not worthy of me, I will declare *myself* to *you*. And precisely because you come to me bringing nothing, with empty hands, I can be *everything* to you. Enter into the joy of your Lord; now you may see face to face what you have formerly believed from afar."

3. HOW FAITH BEGINS

> And there was a woman who had had a flow of blood for twelve years, and who had suffered much under many physicians, and had spent all that she had, and was no better but rather grew worse. She had heard the reports about Jesus, and came up behind him in the crowd and touched his garment. For she said, "If I touch even his garments, I shall be made well." And immediately the hemorrhage ceased; and she felt in her body that she was healed of her disease. And Jesus, perceiving in himself that power had gone forth from him, immediately turned about in the crowd, and said, "Who touched my garments?" And his disciples said to him, "You see the crowd pressing around you, and yet you say, 'Who touched me?'" And he looked around to see who had done it. But the woman, knowing what had been done to her, came in fear and trembling and fell down before him, and told him the whole truth. And he said to her, "Daughter, your faith has made you well; go in peace, and be healed of your disease."
>
> *Mark 5:25–34*

This woman plays less than a minor role in the New Testament; one might say that she belongs among the statistics. I can never remember hearing a sermon on this text. It frequently stood under a cloud as far as the interpreters of Scripture were concerned, for they considered it to be an atrocious miracle tale, full of superstition and magic. They asked themselves in annoyance how such a story could ever have slipped into the New Testament.

Even the context seems to testify to the secondary nature of this anecdote. Our text pops up in the middle of the account of Jairus's daughter. While that main event is occurring, this woman dashes onto the stage for a brief moment. Her name doesn't appear on the program. She remains anonymous. For one second she steps forward out of the crowd and the spotlight sweeps across her; the next moment she steps back and with equal swiftness disappears in the dark.

Is it this "statistic" who is to be dragged out of obscurity two thousand years later and held up to rational moderns for scrutiny? Aren't there other texts in this book which soar above us like mountain peaks and which would be worthier objects of our scrutiny? Why, some may think, doesn't he speak on "Faith, hope, and love," or "In the beginning was the Word," or ". . . the deed" instead of this strange little lady with an indefinable female complaint? Why does he wander off into trivia?

And yet whenever I read this story it stirs me in a special way. The wallflowers on the border of this remarkable book are often especially precious. And that is no surprise. For in the chronicles of ancient history Jesus Christ himself has a minor role; he is an actor on the extreme periphery of the world stage.

The fact that this woman appears in the midst of a shoving crowd underlines even further the secondary character of the scene. When one ponders what has brought these people together, one can only propose a whole batch of motives. The conclusions would certainly be similar to those concerning contemporary mass gatherings: first and foremost, Jesus of Nazareth is a sensation, and everyone has to be there when that legendary and renowned figure makes a personal appearance. But there is something else beyond that. Among this concentrated curiosity of the crowd there are also others who are seeking a last way out of their despair from this Nazarene. They are the sick, who no longer have any hope; the lonely, who seek to catch his eye; and certainly those who long for a helpful word regarding the unsolved problems of their lives.

If we make the somewhat foolhardy attempt to put ourselves in Jesus' place, we might well suppose that this response from the broadest strata of society is not unwelcome to him. If he wants to carry out his task and proclaim God's lordship over this world, then he must have the approval of these people, he needs the uproar and mass movement. Therefore he cannot be indifferent to this crowd cheering him and concentrating all its powers of trust and hope upon him. With such support one can win battles, provided one prepares it properly and strikes while the iron is hot.

But that is the marvelous thing about him. While he is buoyed by the confidence of the crowd, while the immensity of his task may be running through his mind and the vast amount of suffering that presses about him looking for help nearly deafens him, the poor, pitiful woman is not too little for him, and the touch of her trembling, outstretched finger is not too insignificant.

How often this scene is repeated in the Gospel: He whom the whole world cannot contain makes himself small enough to enter into the loneliness of one single human brother and then to be there to such an extent that it seems only he, he alone, only you and I were left in the whole world. For in these men who surround him and whom he could arouse to any sort of power seizure, Jesus Christ sees more than cogs in the great machine of world renewal; they mean more to him than human material submitting to his will to power. In each of them he sees his Father's child, whose unhappiness oppresses him, whose sorrow clutches his throat, and whose guilt burdens his own heart. That is the reason he can be available to that little old lady, that is why the lights go down on all the other people and only these two figures—as if they alone existed—fill the entire stage: the Savior of the world and this *one* person who needs him enough to make a crazy, mixed-up attempt to come in contact with him.

Why do I say she was mixed up?

Well, it is clear that at first she has no idea of who Jesus of Nazareth is. She uses no sort of title to address him (such as "Jesus, thou son of David," or even "thou Son of God"), so we cannot assume that she has even the vaguest notion about whom she is addressing. Much less does she recite a confession of faith; she is, confessionally speaking, completely untutored. Nor do we hear that she had listened to Jesus' proclamation and had been captivated by it; in fact, there is nothing to show that she even *knew* that this Nazarene possessed the words of life and that he was therefore able to comfort men and to turn their hearts. One may say that her reasons for being in that crowd were completely wrong. The simple rumor that this man possessed marvelous powers was enough to prompt her to give him a try. After all, she had had bad luck with doctors; she didn't want any more to do with them, whether quacks or professionals. So she ran to this "magnetic healer" from Nazareth in order to expose herself to the radiation of his healing power.

That is exactly what still happens hundreds of times every day. The incurable seek a last chance in the healing art of the occult or semioccult. As the followers huddle together in the waiting-room and exchange their stories, mass suggestion sees to it that they are well prepared to experience the great miracle.

To put it mildly, this woman is operating under a terrific misunderstanding when she comes to Jesus with this in mind.

Her misunderstanding betrays itself in a whole series of telltale signs. Jesus can only come to a person and help him when that individual achieves personal fellowship with him. This woman, however, doesn't want a personal relationship; she is intent on remaining an anonymous atom in the crowd. For that reason she does not step up to him in face-to-face encounter; she moves in on him from behind. She is not interested in his face or in his message. She only wants the magic contact with his robe that will shower her with the sparks of healing power. That is the second misunderstanding; she lives in the thought-world of primitive magic. She believes that a single touch with her finger will complete the circuit of magical radiation. In other words, this woman moves within the tenacious thought-patterns of heathendom. She is caught in the categories of magic and superstition. We see her as so undescribably primitive that she never once notices the contradiction between that twilight world of the occult and the world of the Old Testament. The Old Testament consistently condemns that specter of magic as blasphemy, and the Old Testament is, after all, "Holy Scripture" to the Man from Nazareth.

It is actually grotesque that, in this woman's eye, Jesus of Nazareth is some sort of enchanted figure from the world of witchcraft. No misunderstanding could be stranger or further from the truth. Even a not-too-bright confirmand could tell her that much.

Her state of anxiety has led her to project a savior-figure, for magic is always a symbol of anxiety. When Faust does not know how to get out of the endless confusion of his despair, he swears allegiance to magic, seeking salvation from Nostradamus. But that only increases his anxiety. For now he lives in constant fear of powers of enchantment, of bondage to hell, of the evil eye, and of the tentacles of evil. Is Jesus of Nazareth to enter this melancholic, comfortless world as a sort of rescue party? Then it would not be at all clear whether he was driving out the devil of anxiety by the power of Beelzebub or whether he himself was not merely *one* demon among others.

It is necessary to think through the misunderstanding in detail like this in order to appreciate the surprising, even crazy, course of events which the text goes on to describe.

Anyone would think that, before Jesus could deal with this woman, he would have to correct her wild ideas. He would need to have a heart-to-heart talk with her about the utter nonsense of magic and about the true nature of his person. Yet nothing like that occurs. He helps her at once, giving her more than she bargained for. He turns to her and speaks words which she never expected to hear. Perhaps he said to himself, "Once this person really understands me and grasps the fact that I am the Savior who brings her into the rescuing love of her Father and mine, then all the mirages, all the dark fantasies, and all the errors of her old life will inevitably fall away, like worn-out clothes."

That is Jesus Christ. He doesn't set forth conditions which I must fulfill before I can find him. He doesn't tell me, "You are looking for me in the wrong way." On the contrary, whenever he notices even a *trace* of hunger and thirst and longing for peace in me, he is there at once—totally and without reservation.

And yet in how many wrong ways we seek him! Naturally it doesn't need to be the way of magic. It can also involve quite different misunderstandings. One of us sees in Christianity a religious mooring for morality that mankind cannot do without. For a society, he may argue, cannot exist without certain commonly agreed-upon standards of value. These values seem to be best preserved through religious indoctrination. Thus Jesus Christ becomes the patron saint of the social order. Or we tell ourselves that, through its message of love, Christianity sees to it that society remains properly humane. Or we say that Christianity watches over the individual and "the infinite worth of the human soul." We need it in an age when the mass threatens to absorb the individual and take away his identity. Or we say that the Judaeo-Christian tradition provides us with the necessary Western ideology to withstand the intellectual challenge of the East.

This whole mock-Christian program that we all recognize, that speaks to us from hundreds of newspaper columns, and that we hear from an equal number of political and cultural speeches—this whole mock-Christian phraseology rests on a horrible misunderstanding of who Jesus Christ really is. For his will is quite different. He wants to bring us home to the peace of his Father and to remove from us everything that stands between us and God. To put it in a quite childlike, uncomplicated, and yet consciously arresting way—he wants to bring us to heaven, and nothing else. And *then* (although only as a subsidiary by-product of this main point) he wants to allow us to share in all the other benefits. In his school he will teach us to understand the infinite worth of the human soul—the individual soul!—because he died for each one of us. And he will also help us to find support in him when we are besieged by false ideologies of redemption. He will even arouse our consciences, providing both state and society with a reservoir of mature persons who know how to find the balance between freedom and order.

But all that, as stated above, only comes to us "beside" and "along with" our *primary* striving after him and his kingdom. When we elevate these by-products into our main concern, and speak of Christianity as a magic potion to be used for restoring trade and commerce to health, and when we predict that without it we will go to the dogs politically and culturally, then it's as though we were running down a track with all the switches thrown the wrong way. For this mock-Christian standpoint can be represented without one's having been laid hold

56

of by Jesus Christ at all. In that case one would represent a so-called Christian body of ideas without needing to believe in Christ oneself. In this way one would have a doctrine of salvation without having a savior. But even though it may be false, and even though we today may be corrupted by this falsehood to the extent that the nonsense about a "Christian West" has become sounding brass and a tinkling cymbal, Jesus Christ simply does not knock all that out of us—just as he did not drive the magic out of that poor woman.

Therefore, if we coolly start from the assumption that Christianity is the foundation of our Western morality and value system, and if this banality is the only thing we know to say about him, then this minimum of Christianity is somehow still the equivalent to that momentary contact which the hemorrhaging woman tried to make with Jesus' robe. To hold such a view means that we have really not yet heard the word of the Savior nor have we yet faced up to him personally in any way. We only have a hold on the very fringe of his robe. But he who is honest in his grasping for that outer fringe and holds tightly to the Savior, at least to that extreme edge, has the promise that Jesus will turn and ask the question, "Who has touched my clothing?"

That is the greatness of Jesus Christ. Long before we have disentangled ourselves from our false presuppositions, he is already present. Long before we feel the touch of his peace, his rescuing arms are already embracing us. And long before we have lost our way and wandered far off, he has caught up with us. He is like a mother who rocks her feverish child in her arms. We just can't get rid of our anxious fantasies. Will our social structures lose all their powers of regeneration and thus tend toward complete collapse or replacement through revolution? Is our life as purposeless as a car in neutral? Are we just spinning castles in the air and drifting farther from our goal? Is the guilt we have incurred a curse which will burden us all our days? Will our children go astray? Could our marriage break up? We live among these anxieties like a feverish child; and that is exactly the way the woman in our text suffered under the hopelessness of her outcast condition and the ghosts of her

57

superstitious mind. And all the time (without her knowing it) the Savior is right there with his peace. All the time he comforts us as a mother comforts her child. His arms enclose us amid all our anxieties. Like a feverish child we feel the nearness of that peace, and yet we do not really know where to find it to make it our own.

So it is quite different from the way it first appeared. Jesus Christ is not a figure from the twilight world of magic. In reality the exact opposite is true. He encompasses this human being together with her enchanted world in the fullness of his peace. When she approaches the Savior, this woman's fever-fantasies subside and her crazy ideas lose their power; it is only a question of time until she notices the difference and rejoices over the new center of her life.

Among all the people that seek him there and crowd around him, Jesus thus finds the *one* person who requires his help and who needs him as his Savior, even though that person has no inkling whatsoever of who or what this Savior is.

But *if* that is so, and if he knows us all far more fully than we realize, then what can be the significance of his question, "Who touched me?" Doesn't he thereby show that he has not yet recognized the person seeking help, and that in fact he doesn't know him at all?

I think that he knew the person who touched him very well, and that he wanted to accomplish something quite different with his question. He demanded that the person who sought him now step forward and let herself be recognized, instead of hiding in the surging mass around him. He required her to step up to him with her need and her cry for help, presenting herself openly and publicly.

Viewed in that light, if we want to approach the mystery of Jesus it is not enough for us to go along with the general usages of Christianity—to participate in the customary baptismal and confirmation services, not to shun a church wedding, and to make a courtesy visit to church once in a while. Christian "business-as-usual" does *not* lift the burden of restlessness and guilt from me, nor does it give me peace. In our story many other people surged around Jesus and were pushed up against his clothing, but not a single one of them left the scene as a new man. Yet one person—or more precisely—one *woman* went away changed, but she had to confess that she needed his help. She had to answer his question, "Who touched me?" She had to show her colors. Even though her illness had already been cured, it would have been of little help. What good is a healing to me if I don't know at whose hands I have received it, or if I fail to discover that the miracle of health is the message of a heart that is mindful of my best interests and that wants to bless my life? How many a man has gone to the dogs precisely because of his good health or because of his recovery from illness! The reason is that no thanks grew out of his experience and he overlooked the message directed to him through the miracle of his health. His robust constitution may only have served to make him thoughtless or even heartlessly brutal about the suffering people around him. Many a man might come to his senses sooner if things went a little worse for him. The fact that her hemorrhaging stopped was not the salvation of this woman. The great transformation and change in her life occurred when she was challenged, when she had to present herself before Jesus to experience him and to hear his rescuing word.

This discovery brings us still closer to the central point of our story. We seek to find this point by means of the following questions: In what did the faith of this woman *consist*? Was there any faith at all beneath the tangle of her unbelief?

To answer this question, we must take a small piece of information into account. According to the Mosaic laws (Lev. 15:25 ff.) a woman with a flow of blood was considered unclean. She was not only unable to participate in cultic activities (and therefore barred from worship services!), but her uncleanness was considered contagious, so that she would be shunned as a leper. Behind these laws stands the idea that illnesses of this sort are the result of sin. We need not concern ourselves here with the question of whether this whole complex of ideas is meaningful or not. We need only establish the fact that this woman lived under such conceptions and was heavily burdened by them. Therefore, we may infer from the text, she was tormented by guilt and anxiety, she was shunned and isolated, she was barred from the comfort of worship services and *she had carried the burden of this ban for twelve long years.* She must have felt like Job, who could still say in the early stages of his misfortune, "The Lord has given and the Lord has taken away," but when no end to the troubles came in sight, what had at first seemed to make sense as testing soured into a caricature of meaninglessness.

Although all that is true, although she must see herself as an outcast, although heaven is closed to her and she stands in limbo, unrecognized and herself recognizing no meaning in life, she still holds fast to one last thought: that One standing there could help you. A tiny spark of confidence still glows in a heart that is nearly burned out. And for the sake of this one little spark that still lives in a heap of ashes, even though it is almost extinguished by the rubble of superstition—for the sake of this *one* little spark, she is rescued.

Perhaps I am a person who has already cooled to the point where I am numb and cannot invest the remainder of my hope in a prayer. Perhaps I am no longer even able to stammer through the Lord's Prayer. I spend my last little store of hope in burrowing through the daily horoscope or in playing the numbers. There is One to whom even this misguided and played-out little spark is not too small. He finds it, turns to me, and lets me know, "You have touched me, the Savior, even though you didn't even realize it." There is no wilderness so desolate in our life that Jesus Christ will not and cannot encounter us there. I can do nothing else than proclaim to all those who lie in the depths or wander about without a shepherd that this is so—that they may look forward to him who waits for them with his surprises.

One final depth in our story remains to be plumbed. When Jesus turned to the woman and she had to show her colors, she began to tremble "and fell down before him, and told him the whole truth." If one is not content with cheap psychological tricks at this point, explaining this trembling as caused by the excitement of the moment and the shock of the miracle, then one must dig a little deeper and rephrase the question as follows: "What in the world is a 'whole truth' that would make a person tremble to confess it?" What enormities must be revealed here? It can hardly be the magical contact with Jesus' healing power. That merely led up to it.

In reality, something quite different is involved. A moment ago I spoke of the time-bound idea that a woman with a flow of blood was considered unclean and that she was therefore shunned. Even the slightest contact would transfer this uncleanness to objects and other people. To that extent she was the bearer of a contagion and people had to be on their guard against her. Therein lay her abysmal loneliness—a loneliness which modern categories are scarcely adequate to measure. Only when we are clear about that will we be able to grasp the frightful and dismay-producing truth that she must confess: By her touch she has made Jesus of Nazareth unclean; she has infected him. More than that, from her magic-oriented point of view, it appeared that when the miracle occurred *she* was suddenly freed from the burden of her uncleanness, but that burden was transferred to *him*. He had taken it over from her.

Since she may have dimly perceived this, she stole upon him from behind with the uneasy feeling that she was doing something monstrous in shifting her uncleanness to another person. It was like crucifying someone in order to get rid of your own cross. And this monstrous deed came to light when Jesus turned upon her. Now do we have some notion of *what* she had to confess? Understanding the charge against her, do we realize that such a monstrous deed could bring people of much sterner stuff to tremble?

What has happened here? We face the unbelievable fact that the message of Jesus Christ suddenly has been marked out on the coordinate system of magic. The diamond of the gospel sparkles in ever new refractions of light.

The joyous news can be presented in the thought-forms of Judaism and also, as happens in the prologue to John's Gospel, in the concepts of Greek philosophy. One can express it in Buddhist words, and a missionary in the African bush can present it in the forms and ideas of primitive magic. Wherever one of his human brothers may find himself, Jesus Christ is directly available. It is a part of the mystery and miracle of Pentecost that everyone, "Parthians and Medes and Elamites," magicians and wise men, Marxists and existentialists, Buddhists and nihilists, can approach him, and that they are all able to hear and express the mighty acts of God in *their* languages. One need not first learn the language of Canaan in order to come to grips with him. One need not first enjoy a Western Christian education in order to understand him. For he comprehends not only the whole earth, he also comprehends the languages and values, the thoughts and feelings of all people. Jesus Christ understands anyone when he expresses his anxiety and his hunger for peace in his own language and concepts. And he even understands us when we no longer have concepts but can only groan and stammer inarticulately as the dying do in their final hour.

At this point we stand before the peculiar miracle of this story, placed like a wallflower on the border of the New Testament. This superstitious woman, within the framework of her very strange and terribly primitive world of ideas, has grasped the mystery of the Savior at a deeper level than many theologians and worldly-wise men. She has made Jesus unclean by touching him. She has thereby saddled him with her suffering and by this bold touch has made him a companion in her affliction. She has had her life's burden taken away by him and has pulled him down into her deep misery. Thus with her poor finger she has unwittingly pointed to the mystery of the cross. She has prophesied something that she herself in her misery can not yet comprehend. For a moment she becomes a sister of that great sinner who pours a costly ointment over Jesus and with it anoints him for burial. Both women have momentarily illuminated the mystery of the cross without themselves realizing it. For the prophet speaks more than he himself knows. Therefore the memory of both of these "unknowing-knowing" women will be preserved as long as the gospel is proclaimed (Matt. 25:13).

This woman made Jesus her brother. In doing so she has made him into precisely what he wants to be for us. That is why he went to the cross. And she trembles because she suddenly realizes just what she has done—nothing less—which appears to her to be mad. She still has qualms that bringing the Son of God down into our own abyss contradicts everything that one naturally considers permissible and appropriate to God.

What she did unwittingly, however, is actually the miracle of the gospel—that there is no depth in which this Savior will not become our brother. We don't have to become different from what we are. Above all, we don't need to become religious in order to come near him. He comes for us wherever we are: in the highways and hedges, in the places where we have dirtied our hands and in the abysses where we suffer our greatest anxieties. He comes for us when we live in the world of Bert Brecht and have learned to see the misery of mankind through his eyes; or when, with Goethe, we experience the dubious nature of all Faustian seeking and struggling; or when we, as the young Nietzsche, see previous values perish and feel we are treading on thin ice. *He comes for us wherever we are.*

And this miracle—that there is such a thing, that there is such a thing at all—this miracle may be experienced, proclaimed, and expressed at every stage of our life. The elderly woman in an old folks' home can do it, and so can a teen-ager who transfers her intense longing for life to film idols. It can be expressed in the bold flow of Pauline theology and also in the primitive ideas of the woman with a flow of blood. The majesty of Jesus is just as close to the *Threepenny Opera* as to a chorale. For *that* is his majesty: to be near to all and a neighbor to everyone, to take our burden upon himself while we become free.

4. HOW CRISES IN FAITH ARISE

Then he [Jesus] made the disciples get into the boat and go before him to the other side, while he dismissed the crowds. And after he had dismissed the crowds, he went up into the hills by himself to pray. When evening came, he was there alone, but the boat by this time was out on the sea, beaten by the waves; for the wind was against them. And in the fourth watch of the night he came to them, walking on the sea. But when the disciples saw him walking on the sea, they were terrified, saying, "It is a ghost!" And they cried out for fear. But immediately he spoke to them, saying, "Take heart, it is I; have no fear."

And Peter answered him, "Lord, if it is you, bid me come to you on the water." He said, "Come." So Peter got out of the boat and walked on the water and came to Jesus; but when he saw the wind, he was afraid, and beginning to sink he cried out, "Lord, save me." Jesus immediately reached out his hand and caught him, saying to him, "O man of little faith, why did you doubt?" And when they got into the boat, the wind ceased. And those in the boat worshiped him, saying, "Truly you are the Son of God."

Matthew 14:22–33

Once when Bismarck entered the room of a friend, he saw his own picture hanging on the wall. Apparently it was somewhat forceful and a little larger than life, as many Bismarck portraits are. The original, however, having confronted this "counterfeit," shook his head. "Is that the way I'm supposed to look? That's not me." He turned around, pointed to a picture on the opposite wall of Peter sinking beneath the waves and said, "That is me."

This picture of Peter sinking beneath the waves is certainly familiar to all of us, be it from the biblical text, from the history of art, or from both. It has touched everyone, calling for the same identification that Bismarck drew: The waves have sometimes been too high for me, too; I too have been immersed in anxiety; and in critical moments I too have cried out, "Lord, help me, I'm sinking!"

Yet even in the midst of such thoughts we cannot avoid picking up a certain amount of static. It arises in our intellect, which acts here as a sort of static transmitter. This transmitter signals "a similarity, but only a similarity and nothing more!" The negative part of this image fits: I am sinking as Peter did. Heaven knows I'm sure of that; I have plenty of proof. But the positive part—the news of a savior-figure who takes me up in his arms and pulls me back from the abyss—where is there anyone who would walk on water and come to me over the floods? You have to believe in miracles to take that at face value. In fact, one has to be *able* to accept a story like that if it is really going to become a comfort to one. Otherwise it remains just a symbolic representation of the crisis I am in— which does nothing, absolutely nothing, for me in the way of help. And the appearance of Jesus in the night of distress becomes a sentimental dream. One would apparently be more honest and above all more brave without such airy nonsense. I have the feeling that I ought to consider this question thoroughly before going on to the exposition of the text.

Can I really base my faith on a miracle story? Of course, if I had experienced something of that sort, if I had touched it with my fingers and seen it with my eyes, then, perhaps. . . . But a long time ago Lessing said with his unblinking honesty, "Miracles that I see with my own eyes and have an opportunity to test personally are one thing; miracles that I only know through *history*, that others claim to have seen and tested, are quite another." And in another place he says that reports of miracles are still far from *being* miracles.

Lessing's concern may be formulated in the following way: If faith is to help me, it must be more certain than those murderous billows and breakers. That is logical! But how can I base the certainty of this faith on something that is itself *uncertain* and possibly only a fairy tale or propaganda? If I take myself seriously and don't want to seek refuge in empty illusions, then I cannot avoid this question. Or can I?

We must push this threatening question still further. Assume for a moment that a miracle story was told to me that was absolutely incontestable from a modern critical point of view.

The testimony of witnesses had been carefully sifted, and the facts of their physical and psychological aspects were attested by expert opinions. In other words, my certainty at least approached the certainty of first-hand experience. Would I then be better off, and would I have a more reliable basis for my belief?

I am afraid that it would be Jesus Christ himself who would keep us from basing our faith on a miracle like that. Why did he criticize the "generation seeking a sign" and again and again refuse to perform a miracle to prove his power and make it easier for the people to believe? Why did he refuse to leap from the pinnacle of the temple to induce faith by a sort of shock therapy? He knew perfectly well, "These people basically want to watch, not to believe. They want to hear the evidence, but they don't want the adventure of a trust that would make them surrender themselves to me for good or ill." "If I perform a miracle," thought Jesus of Nazareth, "I can win entrance to their nervous system, but I can in no way reach their heart. And that's the only thing I'm concerned about—the heart!" Thus sometimes, after he had performed a miracle and let his majesty shine forth for a moment, he immediately forbade the eyewitnesses to tell anyone else. He didn't want men to fall under the suggestion of a general miracle hysteria to the extent that they would equate a certain feverish mentality—which modern "soul-winners" know how to induce—with "faith." Jesus intended that men become healthy and renewed through an encounter with his own person, that they take his words, "Your sins are forgiven," to heart, that they recognize the presence of the Father in him and come from restlessness to peace, from the far country to their home.

No one has as conclusively rejected miracles as Jesus himself, as soon as they threatened to become *substitutes for faith.* And yet all who met him knew that nothing less than a miracle had happened to them, and that from then on they would live under the spell of that miracle. Looking backward, as they came away from his presence, they suddenly knew that it had been a miracle when he pulled them free from the sin-

66

guilt cycle and bondage to their burdened past, when he gave them a new future, and (the most unlikely of all) when he declared God's grace to them and brought them out of their anxiety-ridden life into the blessedness of being carefree children of their heavenly Father. And when the great disruptions of creation, when sickness and death fell back before him, when the lame man lifted himself from his bed, and when dead eyes reopened, that was something different from a purely medical phenomenon which anyone else could also produce. Those events were like signal fires which announced the coming kingdom of God, already present and victorious in this *one* man. People knew that they had been touched by the finger of God himself when Jesus of Nazareth laid his hand on them. They learned that he was not a teacher like the others, but that he was the great transformer, that he could break chains, loosen entanglements, and give a totally new being. It was enough to take their breath away.

Now they were no longer confronted with a dark, black wall, their life was provided with new meaning; they obtained some notion of what it meant to be right with God and to know the shepherd's presence in the valley of the shadow.

Certainly no one who has experienced the overwhelming power of this new life has been able to keep it to himself. He has to tell others. And since Jesus takes hold of persons in every depth of their being, since he enlightens their understanding, motivates their will, and even animates their feelings, their *imagination* also joins in their praise of this unspeakable gift. It takes that very real experience and expands upon it poetically in order to express the characteristics of his glory by an everchanging pattern of images.

Then what difference does it make if this witness of faith may also have gathered legendary elements? Precisely because the miracle of faith is so fascinating and revolutionary, it seeks to express itself in ever new forms. It uses the matter-of-fact report of the eyewitness who must tell over and over what he experienced with Jesus. It uses song and all kinds of music; it builds cathedrals that reach heavenward; it sinks into wood and stone. And it also employs poetry and legend in order to testify to the *one* miracle in constantly changing ways, describing the mystery of that miracle from all possible angles.

To everyone who receives this testimony, no matter whether he reads the Bible, opens a hymnal, or lets the confession of art speak to him—to everyone who is touched by any of these media comes the moment, no matter what the circumstances, when he simply loses interest in the question of whether this or that report corresponds to a certain event with photographic accuracy and exact objectivity. Instead of that approach he begins to ask the decisive and really relevant question: *What experience of faith is described here?* What real miracle of faith has happened to people to make them recount this or that story? To *what* do they want to testify? *What* are they trying to say? That is the right way to put the question. We shall use this approach to guide us as we feel our way into the message of this text.

The story begins with Jesus making his disciples board a boat so that he can free himself from the pressing crowd and go alone into the mountains to pray.

That is typical of him. Although he is present to help, heal, comfort, and guide others, he does not become totally identified with his work. He is the opposite of the mere "manager." Before he speaks to men he has already talked it over with his Father. He always comes from silence when he breaks into speech. Therefore the air of eternity is about him, and men feel that he comes from somewhere else. The rest of us, even we Christians, often think, "First I do this or that daily task, because that is my job, that is the way I earn my money. And only when I have taken care of this fundamental reality can I devote myself to the religious sector of life, thereby either deepening my daily work a little or completely surmounting it." Jesus, however, knows that the decisive switches are thrown in that conversation with the Father, and then everything that I do, every step I take, every word I say, is only a logical consequence.

Now at night the disciples are alone with the elements on the lake. They run into trouble. On a small scale they experience beforehand what the church has had to cope with on a continuing basis since Good Friday, Easter and the Ascension. The Lord is absent, he has withdrawn out of sight and is barely believable. Meanwhile we feel forsaken and alone; we must see to it that we stay above water and deal promptly with anything that knocks a hole in our little boat or that threatens to sink it.

Anyone who has lived through a ticklish situation at sea knows how it goes: The crew runs from stem to stern, from port to starboard, commands are shouted, pipes shrill across the deck, the excitement vents itself in salty curses, and if anyone makes a mistake, everyone else jumps on him. Every sense is strained, and each moment is packed with decisions, adjustments and physical activity. Is that any time for pious thoughts or hymn-singing? We can do that later (we may think), once we're out of this mess.

Every day we simple landlubbers run into similar times of distress which absorb the last ounce of our energy. We all know situations like that. What a time! Day after day we have to collect our thoughts, or else everything goes to pieces. The potatoes threaten to burn when I take my eye off them for a minute to answer the door, where I am detained by the chatter of a salesman, and just then Aunt Amanda pays me a quick visit. Most of the time I must try to do three things at once. Anyone who manages a large company equipped with several receptionists, often has the feeling that he not only has to direct, but that he also has to play the violin, blow the trombone, and dash off a few runs on the piano in order to keep things in line. We are well aware of everything that we have to keep in mind, and we also know how the constant round of thinking can wear us down and leave us without a word to say. Do we have any brain cells left over for the process of faith to use? Isn't every thought about God a deviation from the current task we have been given? When bombs are bursting around us, or even when we are in the working-day harness, we have no time for extra thoughts. And faith, after all, *is* a thought—or is it?

Certainly everyone has had that experience. And if faith is taken seriously, that experience can make us miserable and sometimes almost tie us in knots. But it is crucial to be clear on this point, because then it becomes apparent that we cannot base our life on our faith. Faith is often conspicuous by its absence. How few moments there are when I consciously recognize that I am performing an act of faith, when I can establish completely, clearly, and unambiguously, "Now I believe." Furthermore, faith is also very unstable. Sometimes on a quiet evening, perhaps after hearing Bach's *St Matthew Passion,* I am completely filled with faith, in fact, I am downright enraptured. If I should die at that moment, heaven's gates would be open wide. But the very next morning it takes only one low blow from an ugly letter to snuff out that feeling again.

No, we cannot base our life on faith. Even the disciples do not live from their faith in that moment when they are battling anxiety and seasickness. They hardly remember that they are believers. There's simply no time to think about it. That may be put very crudely, but that's how it is nevertheless! At that moment the disciples do not live from the fact that God is in their thoughts (because he is not!), but they live because *Jesus Christ* is thinking of them, and the stillness that surrounds his conversation with the Father is filled with these thoughts about his own. Our faith's grip on the Father may loosen. But he in whom we believe holds us fast in his grasp. Jesus' high-priestly prayer does not stop even when we quit praying. Thus, there is really no such thing as "Psychology of Religion" because the decisive events between God and me do not happen in my psyche, my consciousness, at all; they occur in the heart of my Lord. Here (and only here) there is constancy and faithfulness; here there is a love that will not let me go, even though my fever chart fluctuates between faith and little faith, between trust and doubt, and no reliance can be placed on my defiant and despondent heart. I don't need to tell you what a comfort it can be to know that, and how that knowledge can help me survive those times when my own faith is cold and empty and dead and a sealed heaven arches above me.

But then comes the "fourth watch of the night" when Christ appears close by our life's little ship. Then comes the time when we are no longer alone, when he is suddenly at hand, when his overwhelming and immense presence stands before us. No person who has entered into relationship with him has found it to be any other way. This fourth watch of the night comes to every one of us.

The text doesn't give us the slightest hint that the disciples were awaiting him, nor does it imply that they doubted him. Apparently they had neither looked for him nor despaired of him. Their time was so occupied with struggling and working that inner processes of this sort just didn't occur. They were so little occupied with him that they were frightened to death when he suddenly stood before them in the dark and stormy night. They didn't recognize him. They thought he was a ghost, a spectral figure, maybe the monstrous product of their overwrought nerves, but in any case a phantom.

Isn't this feature of our text somewhat typical of what we have all experienced with God? How many of the frightful things we have met in our life were secret messages sent to us by God and delivered to us by him. But we didn't recognize him. Perhaps we met a man—naked, imprisoned, hungry, needing us—but we drew back without recognizing in him the brother of our Savior. The fact that he was wasting away with cancer offended and reminded us of our own frailty. The sad or sullen girl who works at the desk next to ours waited in vain for a kind word to thaw the ice tongs around her heart; she made me so cold and miserable that I avoided her. In all of these encounters the fourth watch of the night had arrived and another was coming to me across the waves. But I was not expecting him to be hidden in a neighbor who was suffering, or even offensive to me; I had no idea that he would be concealed in an experience that rushed down upon me like the stroke of doom. I was intent on meeting God in a hymn, the sound of an organ, or in pious feelings. Every movie director knows what edifying comfort those things can produce in theater goers. But I had no idea that the Lord of my life would appear in such a disguise, that he would step into my life so alienated and phantomlike, that he would set me tasks and send me messages whose blessing was so thoroughly concealed.

We would let all these fourth night-watches in our life pass by unnoticed and without effect if he himself did not say to us, "Fear not, it is I!" We never recognize the Lord by his outward appearance. Outwardly he is always hidden; he is either disfigured by rags and sores, or he is transfigured as he was on Easter morning when he comes to us. We recognize him only by his *voice* when he tells us, "Fear not, it is I!" When we hear this address amid our perplexity, when we hear that our anxiety shall be taken away, that there is someone who is stronger than the distressing elements, and that a refuge from all storms and loss has been provided for us, then we know that he himself is present.

Peter is fascinated by this moment. For the first time he has experienced what it is like to be able to know the presence of the Lord in this way. It is no different for us today. Whoever senses his protecting hand in the midst of life's terrors and experiences the miracle of suddenly being no longer alone knows something of this electrifying newness that has come into his life. He feels a real sense of curiosity, a desire to experiment with this new element. He senses that it is an exciting situation to be a Christian.

Suddenly Peter not only loses his terror of the foaming fierceness and impact of the waves, but he even wants to play with the elements and see for once just how far a man can go with his faith. He gets the itch to try an experiment: "Lord, if it is you, bid me come to you."

During the war a theologian friend of mine unceremoniously attacked the then ruling powers by totally ignoring various strict regulations—for example, a prohibition against speaking in public which was placed on him—and made not the slightest effort to conceal his opposition. One time one of us said to him in friendly concern and also a bit in jest, "Dear friend, you have a positively breathtaking trust in God. You seem to me to be like Daniel in the lions' den, walking around unconcerned among the beasts. But aren't you going too far? God has indeed promised us that we really need not have any fear of the beasts. But you are pushing your trust in God a little far. You are just about pulling the lion's beard and stepping on his tail. Must one push faith that far? Is that faith any more? Isn't that really tempting God like a mischievous little boy?"

I still remember exactly how my friend answered that. He said, "Maybe you are right. The experience of how God leads me day by day, pulling me through every difficult situation and neatly protecting me, does in fact strike me as an adventure. And sometimes I ask myself if that is still faith or if it hasn't gone over into a quite human dare-deviltry.".

In exactly the same way Peter is living through the first fascinating experience of a man who senses that everything is transformed and all perspectives changed when one begins to take Christ into account. He challenges his Lord in order to test out how far faith can support him—even over the water.

All that is downright fantastic. If a student should ask me during a discussion period whether he should test his faith by walking across the nearest river, I would certainly rap him on the knuckles and warn him against an enthusiastic, mixed-up theology. I would tell him, "What you want is not 'proper' for a Christian; it is either foolishness or the result of a neurosis."

But Jesus Christ doesn't rap Peter's knuckles; he approves his disciple's somewhat eccentric experiment. Perhaps he rejoices that for once someone wants to test out his faith cheerfully, completely without theological brakes and uninhibited by reflection. Those who are too bright theologically, who meditate too long on *what* they pray and *how far* they ought to go in their prayers, and who, out of pure anxiety over demanding something impossible from God, end up by saying only "Thy will be done," ultimately have no confidence in God at all. Their pious self-denial is probably only a spiritual vitamin deficiency. Their theological inhibitions are in reality only expressions of their little faith.

For that reason the Lord loves Peter, resolutely prepared as he is for search, risk, and even letdown. A false theology of faith is certainly less displeasing to God than a correct, chemically pure orthodoxy that is ice-cold at bottom and that clips the wings of an adventurous faith. It is heartwarming to see that Jesus, perhaps not without a trace of affectionate and kindly humor, does not roar out through the stormy night with

73

a theological lecture on the nature of faith, but that he simply says, "Good, come on, walk on the water!"

Why is it, then, that Peter fails and goes under? It would certainly be wrong for us to formulate the answer of our text to that question as follows: "Peter mixed up faith and monkey business. He both did and believed the wrong thing." Whether his faith was false is a question which our story leaves completely unanswered. It doesn't deny that his faith was wild and reckless, independent of all that is normally considered Christianity by churchly, middle-class folk. But Peter's failure has a totally different cause. One single factor made him fail: he looked at the waves instead of the Lord. When that huge mass of water poured over him and the H_2O beneath him gave way, when he got his first mouthful and started to cough, then his faith fled and he could no longer see the figure of the Lord. *That* was his disaster.

For basically faith is nothing else than a certain way of looking at things. A single false glance can be enough to make me fall into the abyss. For example, if I look at what the existential philosophies call "possibility," if I consider all the complications and dangers that *could* press in upon my life— what *would* possibly occur if I failed the examination, what *would* happen if my heart trouble led to an attack, if my boss retired soon and a new one *should* come, if the child we are awaiting *should* be deformed, if Berlin *might* not be able to hold out any longer, if the Chinese *should* use the hydrogen bomb— if I look at all these threatening possibilities that face me, then I am sucked into the maelstrom of anxiety and the water gets in my windpipe. Then *that* is my personal disaster.

That is why the Lord warns repeatedly against an anxious spirit. For being anxious has meant what happens to Peter in this story. It means that I look at the waves instead of at the Lord who walks upon them. But if I keep my eye on that Lord, the water and spray are still there, to be sure, but cannot do a thing to me any more. For I am held by him whom the wind and waves obey, who not only is the guide of human hearts but also is master of the natural elements, who not only comforts in sickness but also can heal the sick.

But suddenly Peter forgets all that. A few minutes earlier he was like the Rock of Gibraltar. It is unbelievable how quickly the clouds can gather and cold and darkness spread where a moment before there was only sunshine, warmth, and a clear sky.

At this point, however, the miracle of the fourth night-watch shines with its utmost brilliance.

Peter's faith has deserted him. But the Lord seizes him and holds him fast. Granted, Peter has only a little faith, but he has a great Lord. "O love, that wilt not let me go!"—that is probably the last thought he can manage. It wasn't much. If the Apostles' Creed had been in existence at that time, he wouldn't have been able to get it together. At that moment the question of whether Jesus was the Son of God, or whether various dogmas were true, was far beyond him; the water was up to his neck and he was more dead than alive. It wasn't much for him to be able to cry "Help" or to know the proper address for this cry and add "Lord." But this minimum, this miserable remnant of his former foolhardiness, is sufficient for Jesus Christ to enter the picture and enfold him in his rescuing arms. For Jesus Christ is greater than our faith. That undergirds our life. He is also greater than everything that would stand between him and us.

Gorch Fock, who was a sailor in World War I, once wrote home, "If you should hear that I have fallen in battle, do not cry. Remember that even the ocean in which my body sinks is only a pool in my Savior's hand." Gorch Fock knew that death or sorrow do not disappear for those who have a Savior. Faith does not in any way excuse us from pains and anguish that are the lot of all mankind. And we Christians are not promised that things will be made easier for us, or that God will provide a sheltered spot for us. Gorch Fock knew that it is frightful to go down with a torpedoed ship and to be strangled by the cold dark vortex. But he knew something more: he believed that the threatening and throttling elements were only a pool in the hand of his Savior. Therefore, no matter where he fell and no matter where he sank, that hand of his Lord surrounded him and would in fact save him. It included both

75

the drowning man and the water in which he sank. And as long as he kept his eye on that hand it was, in a higher sense, immaterial to him whether he went over the waves or was swallowed by them.

We don't know what destiny is reaching out for us in the remaining years of this decade, but one thing we do know: that hand reaches out for us, too. That is the message of this story. And how can it be said more relevantly or more precisely than by means of sinking Peter—Peter who is none other than I, with my fever chart of a great "little faith," with my anxiety and my curiosity, with my experience that God is always greater than my heart and that he stays true to me when I am false to him? And then after all the storms are over, and the sea is smooth once again; when calm weather returns, and I once more come to myself; then may things turn out as they did with the disciple, who could only fall to his knees and stammer, "Truly you are the Son of God."

Maybe I have other words, not nearly so rich, to state who Jesus is for me. Maybe I only come up with, "I don't know who you are, Jesus of Nazareth, but you are different from all the rest of us. I will dare to hold to you. Then I will have secure footing when all around me gives way." That is not put as fully or as richly as it is stated in the liturgy and the catechism. Yet Jesus Christ would hear it, and for him it would be enough.

5. WHAT THE WORD "FAITH" MEANS

And Jesus went away from there and withdrew to the district of Tyre and Sidon.

And behold, a Canaanite woman from that region came out and cried, "Have mercy on me, O Lord, Son of David; my daughter is severely possessed by a demon."

But he did not answer her a word.

And his disciples came and begged him, saying, "Send her away, for she is crying after us."

He answered, "I was sent only to the lost sheep of the house of Israel."

But she came and knelt before him, saying, "Lord, help me."

And he answered, "It is not fair to take the children's bread and throw it to the dogs."

She said, "Yes, Lord, yet even the dogs eat the crumbs that fall from their master's table."

Then Jesus answered her, "O woman, great is your faith! Be it done for you as you desire." And her daughter was healed instantly.

Matthew 15:21–28

The statement of Jesus, "Great is your faith," makes us sit up and take notice, for there is literally no one who doesn't long for a great faith. Each one of us has a consuming desire to hold on to some ultimate in his life with absolute certainty. We want to be able to entrust ourself to it, to be able to confess, "I have something upon which I stand or fall. It fills me and supports me; it gives life to my soul, and I could not exist without it." In this form the question about a great faith, about the ultimate ground of our existence, occurs in every human heart. Naturally this form of the question about faith is still broad, general, and vague; it is not posed in "Christian" terms at all. But it is there.

There is still another variation on this question about faith. It is somewhat more definite. It comes from people who are troubled by the whole complex of what is called "church" and "Christianity." They want to get things straight and make a decision. Such people, who are standing on the fringe but want to be in the center and don't yet know how to get there, have asked me again and again, "What exactly is 'faith'? How in the world does a person know whether he has faith? Is it a feeling, an absolute certainty, an illumination—or what? In other words, am I now really a 'Christian'? Am I 'in,' so to speak, or am I some sort of indefinable creature, neither fish nor fowl, that slinks around in the forecourts and the gates of the church but yet does not belong to it—in fact, does not even know where he belongs? Who is the real me?"

I think about a young man, visibly upset, who told me, "I certainly want to believe; I envy all those who know where they stand. But I can't get away from those dogmas, 'born of the Virgin Mary . . . resurrected from the dead . . . ascended into heaven. . . .' That is Greek to me, and I would be ashamed of myself if I simply forged ahead, repressing these intellectual scruples in order to fulfill a longing at the price of dishonesty. I know what you're going to say to me (I was obviously not the first Christian with whom he had discussed the problem); you will probably remind me about the passage of the Gospel about 'Blessed are they who hunger and thirst after righteousness. . . .' Heaven knows I have that hunger, but frankly, it hasn't blessed me. To believe means more than thirsting, it means to be able *to drink* of the eternal spring. The mere longing for that spring lies well below the minimum standard of existence for faith—or does it?"

And a coed asked me the same sort of question. She said, "Faith is supposed to be a support, and I believe I even know why: It makes it possible for me to accept even the difficult and incomprehensible things in my life as coming from a kindly hand. But look, for me, I'm sorry to say, it is all turned around. When I go home in the evening after a concert, it's easy for me to believe that a dear Father rules above the canopy of stars. But when things go badly for me and I am most in need of that relationship with the Father, that's precisely when it stops and I am left completely alone in the rain. That's when God is silent. And a faith that repeatedly shatters against that wall of silence can't be faith, can it? The mere longing for faith is not yet faith, is it?"

What kind of remarkable process or remarkable possession is it to have a "great faith"? This brings us to the theme of our text.

Jesus never told any of his disciples, "Great is your faith." And yet they had left everything for his sake. He had said it to only one other person, and that was another minor figure without a name, the heathen centurion from Capernaum (Matt. 8:5).

What, then, had this woman done to make Jesus praise her faith like that? Only this: she came to Jesus and stretched out her hands to him.

There are people enough today who exactly like the young man I just mentioned cannot make their peace with this or that "dogma." They are pulled to and fro by their doubts. They ought to open their ears and hear about that "great faith." For that faith does not consist in "believing something is true" or in some sort of special antenna for religious questions. It consists in a struggle, a conversation with God.

It is very easy to discover how such a conversation with God proceeds. There is calling, or rather crying, aloud; there is discussion; the need is laid before God, there is silence. There are dangerous pauses and moments come when understanding breaks down; crises arise and every moment we think, "Now one of us will get up and leave"; finally fellowship is established and Jesus Christ rises to give me his hand for time and eternity, saying, "Be thou whole, faithful child."

All of it is in this conversation: silence, rejection, moments of suspense, acceptance.

People who want to speak like this with Jesus can identify with today's text. Let us now discuss this profound, even unfathomable account from the New Testament.

How did it begin? How did the woman come to Jesus?

It says simply, "A Canaanite woman from that region came out." Even these innocent words have their impact. Because in coming she has to overcome prejudices that her people harbored

79

against the person of the Nazarene. She must figuratively cross the border of an alien land. She must enter an environment that in values and outlook is separated by an abyss from all she holds near and dear. It is almost as if a present-day Arab would slip over into hostile Israeli territory in order to visit a famous man. And ultimately there was a note of risk in her coming. After all, she only knew of him by hearsay, and that rumor could have deceived her. She could have been badly duped, so she risked not only going home disappointed, but also being accused of going on a fool's errand.

But that's the way every faith begins. One must dare to come to Jesus even at the risk of being disappointed. Had the woman stayed at home and therefore not ventured to cross the border, had she told herself that there was no point in going, then Jesus would be no less the Christ; but she would never have entered the sphere of his blessing and would have remained hopeless and alone.

It is no different with us. We have to cross the boundary of two thousand years to reach the figure of the Nazarene. We live in a world of supersonic flight, computers, and artificial satellites. Are we to entrust ourselves and our questions about life to a man who rode a donkey in a legendary far-off time in a corner of the world and had as little notion of our problems— of *my* problems—as Diogenes did about the construction of a modern skyscraper? Moreover, we must also cross the boundary of the great and clamorous events around us and plunge into the deep stillness that surrounds Jesus—a stillness that nevertheless has moved and shaken the world more than all our moon rockets and all our noisy conferences between East and West.

Thus she came to Jesus. But she did not complete her mission as quickly as she probably had planned. There are tests, pauses, and silence. Luther said that the woman first had to endure some "hard knocks" before she was given help. Despite her despairing plea (remember, it concerned her child!) Jesus is silent: "But he did not answer her a word." The silence of God is the greatest test of our faith. Who is not aware of that?

Just like this woman and all the rest of us, John the Baptist questioned and criticized when he was in prison. It is a great comfort to realize that we poor people of the twentieth century are not the only ones who seem to be God-forsaken questioners when we suffer under the silence of God. Even John the Baptist rebelled against this silence of Jesus. "How long are you going to keep us in suspense? If you are Christ, say so! Let a voice from heaven say that you are! Don't you notice that your silence upsets us? Don't you see how much more merciful it would be if that *one* voice would ring out? Then men would have to hear instead of being stretched on the rack by your silence and thrown into the torment of uncertainty. Why this continual limping between faith and doubt? Why don't you set things straight, God?"

Human beings are just not able to remain silent that long about what is happening. They can't look at that much blood. They can't listen that long to the cries of the unfortunate. But does that make them more merciful? Obviously not. The disciples are precisely that sort of person for whom Jesus' silence lasts too long. They can't take the woman's misery. But that doesn't make them one bit more merciful. The woman clearly feels that too, otherwise she would have turned to the disciples in their new mellow and helpful mood. But she knows that the disciples are not at all merciful when they give in to her cry for help. They just have weak nerves. Such people are often considered especially sympathetic and neighborly, because they are yielding and inclined to smooth things over. But they are not one bit more merciful. Even the hosts of cripples and beggars I saw along the road in the Orient did not believe in the pity of men, otherwise they would not have displayed their sores and mutilations so openly in order to touch stony hearts.

The woman prefers holding to the silent Jesus rather than depending on mankind. Obviously God's silence must be measured by different standards than those applied to the silence of men. The Canaanite woman reaches *behind* that silence. She realizes,

> Judge not the Lord by feeble sense,
> But trust him for his grace;

> Behind a frowning Providence
> He hides a smiling face.[1]

The same thing applies to God's silence in response to our prayers. Behind the darkness are higher thoughts of our good, stone after stone of God's plan for the world is being added to our life's plan, even when we see our life only as a confused jumble of stones and shards thrown together under a silent heaven. How many senseless blows of fate fall on us here below! Here we live, suffer, suffer *injustice*, die, are massacred, done in anonymously—and all of it under a silent heaven that never says a word about it.

The cross was the greatest silence of all. There the night of darkness dispatched its last troops against God's Son; the demons were released and the ugliest instincts since Adam unchained. But God said nothing about it. Only a dying man cried aloud in that silence and asked why—yes, why—God had forsaken him. God still remained silent, when even dumb nature began to speak by a shuddering gesture and the sun withdrew its light. The constellations cried out but God was silent. Yet it is precisely at this point that the great secret of that silence conceals itself. This very hour, when God gave no word, no syllable of an answer, was the great turning point of world history. This was the hour when the veil of the temple tore and God's heart was opened to us with all his surprises. By being silent God was suffering too; by being silent he entered with us into the brotherhood of death and the deep valley, knowing all about it and (while we thought he knew nothing of it or even was dead) doing his loving work behind the dark curtains. The silence of that night on Golgotha is the basis for our life. What would we be without the cross? What would we be without the knowledge that God sends his Son to us in the silent abysses and dark valleys, that he becomes our companion in death—while his "higher thoughts" are already pressing on mightily toward Easter, there to bring us fulfillments of which we have no notion.

Truly, God's silence is different from the silence of men. As

1. William Cowper, "God moves in a mysterious way."

Jesus lay in the ship, sleeping and silent, he was kinder and his helping hand was nearer and surer than the disciples in their anxious shouting ever realized. There is no silence of indifference in God (nor in Jesus); there are only those higher thoughts—and not for one minute a silent fate. The woman who comes to Jesus knows that. Therefore she waits out the silence and never draws back her outstretched hands.

Now comes the second "hard knock," bringing a fresh test of faith. The silence is suddenly broken. Out of the indistinct conversation two sentences can be heard: first, "I was sent only to the lost sheep of the house of Israel," and then, "It is not fair to take the children's bread and throw it to the dogs."

That means, in a quite straightforward and apparently brutal way, "You don't belong to the one group of children who have been entrusted to me."

Between these two dark sentences rings the single outcry, "Lord, help me!" but this shrill outcry is muffled and apparently choked by the power of the divine silence.

What did Jesus intend by his reply? First of all, there is an historical allusion involved. Part of the structure of the divine plan of salvation was that Jesus' work should begin with the people of Israel. The leverage was to be applied at that lowest point of the great weight of humanity, to that "stubborn and stiffnecked people" (Lessing). Only when that was done and completed should his work extend farther. Yet this first task was not finished. The "nations," all the rest of humanity, were not yet eligible for their turn. Thus there is a sense in which Jesus was not "there" for that woman. He was still not "available" to her. In other words, this woman had to realize, "God is indeed good, but he is not good *to me*. Jesus Christ is indeed the Savior, but he is not *my* Savior. There is indeed something called the 'communion of saints,' but I don't belong to it."

Haven't we all had a similar experience at one time? Perhaps many a person could agree. "How kind that remote Jesus of Nazareth is! I would indeed like to live in his peace. In difficult times his kind words have been like a mother's hand stroking my brow and making things all right again." These words today may produce an effect like the Easter bells did on Faust, when, in a very dangerous and despairing moment of his life, he was about to drink poison; suddenly he heard the Easter bells, and they surrounded him with magic memories of his childhood home. For many these words may be a similar comfort, or even a similar enchantment, greeting them from afar.

But then comes the inescapable knowledge, "I don't belong." Why not? Because there are so many unsolved riddles about his person. Because of the cross, because of the resurrection, because of the "dogmas." How happy I would be to live in his peace, but I am not satisfied with this or that about the church or about most Christians. Granted, I would like to apply his kind words to myself like balm, but I don't want to take in all the rest along with them. Finally (and this is probably the ultimate misgiving that keeps people from daring to count themselves Christian), could I maintain my Christian allegiance if it was attacked from all sides, if God so shockingly and continually seemed to lose out and human defiance reigned supreme, if belief in love and righteousness was continually compromised, and if the dear Father above the canopy of stars turned out to be a childish dream? Could I endure all that? Happy the man to whom faith is given in such measure that he can endure all that. But it wasn't given to *me*, "*I* don't belong."

How many would say, like the Canaanite woman, "I don't belong, I *cannot* belong"? And many think they know *why* they don't belong. They say, "It all depends on whether or not you can believe. Either you *have* this faith or you don't have it. Either you have some sort of religious 'gift' or you are denied it. I simply can't believe because I don't have the gift; I am excluded. Lucky are those who do!"

I remember the many roads I have marched with good comrades during the war and many an evening we have spent in camps. Or I remember meditative periods on deck under silent southern skies. Time and again the evening conversations about the person of Jesus concluded with those words, "I don't belong." I can see those good companions in my mind's eye.

One could tell that, when speaking about Jesus of Nazareth, they were gazing from afar into a land from which they considered themselves excluded. "You know," one of them said, "it's not for me; I'm not the type. I would like to believe what you believe; I feel that the road you are taking is the right one. But you must leave me behind; I'm made out of different stuff. I don't belong." At this moment I can see them all—those companions of many conversations. Many people of a similar spirit may read this and say, "I don't have the 'gift.' I don't belong." If you think or feel this way, take note of the readiness of that woman—that woman who not only *thought*, but was *told* by a final authority, "You don't belong." How did she manage? Where did that woman find the "great faith" to conquer that rebuff? In no way did it come from the fact that she had a special talent for swallowing difficult dogmas and compulsory articles of faith (we hear nothing about that). Nor did the faith consist in a special religious or metaphysical talent that she possessed. Nor was she so uncritical and intellectually innocent that she simply dropped all her misgivings or repressed them.

Her faith consisted in nothing else than her firm confidence, until the contrary was proved, that Jesus could help her; she could not do otherwise than to call upon him and to hunger and thirst for him as Savior.

To discover something of this hunger and thirst for that high and helpful figure, to give in to it and follow after Jesus—that is already faith. Aren't precisely the hungering, the thirsting, and the homesick praised by Jesus and called "blessed"? Didn't he cry out his "woes" over those who, because of the fullness and certainty of their correct beliefs, were no longer ready to confess, "Nothing in my hand I bring"? Persons who have a hungering heart and a broken spirit are the favorites of God.

There are two ways to deal with this hunger and thirst, with this longing that we all know (and it is important to understand that). We can suppress this longing and hungering for peace, instead of letting it out. We can repress it and kill it with the joys and cares of our daily busy-work. We can even let it be obscured by a TV screen or by the constant flood of

How to Believe Again

popular music the way one ultrapowerful radio transmitter cancels out another.

Or we can dare to go to Jesus as simply as that woman did. We should accept this risk, for it is a fact—Augustine said it once—that "we would not be able to seek God if he had not already found us." The reason that the woman did not give up was because the Lord did not give up—amid his silence.

The conversation continues. The next moment it reaches its climax. Everyone holds his breath. How will the woman react, now that Jesus has said, "Between us stands a wall"? Will this mother really speak about her need? Will she hold up her "great faith" as a sort of letter of recommendation or will she act like a cripple at the roadside and take a chance on the sympathy of God? Will she fall into what Walter Flex once called the "prayer panic of the coward"? Will she begin to cry and turn on the tears? No, something totally unexpected, something tremendous happens. She says, "Yes, Lord." That means, "I must admit you are right when you remain silent. You are totally correct in passing me by. It is not a foregone conclusion that you will help me. You have the right to pass me by, Jesus of Nazareth. I have no claim upon you."

It is good to clarify the immense significance of this thought. For it means nothing less than this: It is not a foregone conclusion that I am accepted by God. It is not a foregone conclusion that you have died on the cross for me. We Christians in Europe and America have gradually accustomed ourselves in a dubious and dangerous way to the idea that the grace of God will be handed to us on a silver platter. Heinrich Heine has spoken this way about God's forgiveness in the cynical phrase: *c'est son métier*, "it's his line." No, forgiveness is not God's line; he is not the official grace-dispenser for mankind, available for help in any situation of life. It is all unutterably different from what a diluted Western Christianity has accustomed itself to taking for granted. The kingdom of God will not be handed us on a silver platter, nor can it be had for the asking. The grace of God can be silent too. We have no claim upon it at all. It can very well happen—and I cannot raise any objection with God—that in my last hour, as I sink into a

86

gloomy night, the *one* person that could accompany me through the dark portal stays away. Jesus Christ is not "in duty bound" to bear my sins and bring me through the black boundary markers of death. The fact that Christ accepts us is anything but a foregone conclusion. And I dare say that no church-going Christian, be he ever so proper, who has not wondered time and again at the fact that he has been shown mercy will enter into the kingdom of heaven. "I deserved nothing but wrath, and am I to be with God in grace?" Am I?

Right now a group is arising among us, composed of young Christians, who are tired of the hollow comforts of existentialism and snobbish aestheticism. They have come home. In some cases they have grown up not even knowing the Lord's Prayer and the Ten Commandments; they have experienced them recently for the first time. Astonishment at the fact that there is a Christ at all is written more clearly and realistically in their eyes than in the eyes of those who come out of surer and more ancient traditions. I mean the astonishment that there really is something other than the great uninvolved Lord God above the heavens and that there is the coming, the forgiveness, and the pain of God as well. Maybe God will have to pull the rug of our satiated Christian West out from under us (as has already happened in the East) in order that we may become similarly astonished Christians when we discover how he can break our fall for us.

All that is involved in that "Yes, Lord." The needy little woman does justice to the grace that can also pass one by. Therefore there can be no question of crying "Woe unto you, you have deceived me."

Now we are approaching the end of this dramatic conversation. The woman continues, "And yet even the dogs get some of the crumbs and pieces that fall from their master's table."

"And yet!" Apparently those words contradict her earlier unconditional assent. Isn't she backing off? Isn't she beginning to become inconsistent?

This inconsistency, if one could call it that, contains the whole mystery of prayer. Exactly the same thing happens in the Lord's Prayer. There we say, "Thy will be done," which is no different from saying "Yes, Lord." And despite this "Yes" we proceed to ask for our daily bread and for many other things. How can this contradiction be explained? As I said before, this confronts us with the deepest mystery of prayer.

After all, we know to *whom* we say "Thy will be done" when we ask God to actualize his will and request that he might bend our wills to conform to it. This prayer "Thy will be done" certainly does not mean that I have to give in absolutely; then one can do nothing; then one becomes a fatalist. No, this "Yes, Lord" is spoken with a joyous undertone, for the woman knows with *whom* she is speaking. And when she says "Yes," that word embodies her entire confidence that he can make things right, as he always does. For this "Yes" is also a yes to the love of Jesus, even if to his hidden love that waits behind his silence. It affirms that love which, despite his passing her by, waits ardently to break forth in majesty and joy, calling his divine "Be thou whole" to his faithful child.

Therefore this woman will not draw back when the night of the cross comes and all others flee. She will not go astray when the persecutions come, when terror reigns, when God meets it all with silence and even the love of the faithful begins to grow cold (Matt. 24:12). Even then she will know that the higher thoughts above the earth are devising ways of peace for her. And because she has the courage to say that "Yes, Lord" she can cheerfully go ahead and ask, ". . . and yet. . . ." This "and yet" can then be interpreted more precisely as, "I have not earned the right to belong to you; I have no claim upon you; you *can* pass me by, O Savior from Nazareth. But will you really do it? Will you manage to pass by a person who threw away all her trump cards—her capacity for living, her moral perfection, and even the trump card of a 'great faith'? Will you be able to pass by a person who turned her back on all those trump cards and on everything else, only to await it all from your love and from your rich hands? Will you manage to do that, O Savior from Nazareth?"

And behold, Jesus cannot. Luther said of this woman, "The woman caught Jesus in his own words"; especially with the words that he loved the hungry, the thirsty, and the poor in spirit, and that he would not despise a contrite heart. The woman did what no one had ever been able to do—she caught the Savior in his own words. She "threw the sack of his promises down at his feet," and the Savior cannot step over that sack.

It wasn't her great faith that conquered. She herself conquered because she took the Savior at his word. She let the heart of God conquer his silence. *That* was why she had a great faith and why one day she will not be the least in the kingdom of heaven.

Therefore we want to absorb this profound story into our own lives and make it come true for us. We want to struggle with the Lord as the Canaanite woman struggled, even when he seems to be silent. We do not want to let him go until he blesses us. We want to show him our empty and longing hands. And he who never gives his children stones for bread, who showed mercy to a poor woman even though she was not a church-going Christian and was heeded by no one, this Lord will also show his mercy to those who do not dare to believe that they are called and chosen but who nevertheless plead moment by moment, "Yes, Lord" and "Have mercy on us."

6. HOW WE LEARN TO SPEAK WITH GOD

Jesus said, "Ask, and it will be given you; seek, and you will find; knock, and it will be opened to you. For every one who asks receives, and he who seeks finds, and to him who knocks it will be opened.

"What father among you, if his son asks for a fish, will instead of a fish give him a serpent; or if he asks for an egg, will give him a scorpion?

"If you then, who are evil, know how to give good gifts to your children, how much more will the heavenly Father give the Holy Spirit to those who ask him?"

Luke 11:9–13

Once in his later years, Lord Melbourne, Queen Victoria's Prime Minister, met the Archbishop of Canterbury. The bishop carried on a conversation with him about the aid and comfort of prayer. "Well," said Melbourne, "I would have only two questions: *To whom* should one pray, and about *what* should one pray?"

Those words express exactly the two basic questions that every thinking man ponders when he lets prayer become a "problem" for him. At this point it doesn't make much difference whether the person is a doubting Thomas or a so-called practicing Christian. Each of them has his particular question on his mind. The doubting Thomas, that is, the skeptic, the secular man, or the atheist, puts the question like this: Suppose for once that there was a God, am I seriously to assert that one can *speak* with him? Wouldn't that be the attempt of an egomaniac to influence God? Doesn't that mean that I grossly overrate myself and that I degrade God to being a puppet of my little miseries and desires? Or in still another way, doesn't that mean that one neglects one's own study of a difficult situation and one's own readiness to take action? Doesn't one then take the easy way of letting "the loving God decide"?

If, therefore, there is supposed to be something called prayer, then at best it can only be a meditative and thoughtful *conversation with yourself*, a "consideration of the world" as Van Buren has expressed it. In that case we lull ourselves into the "illusion" that we have a heavenly partner for our conversation who is listening to us.

Perhaps, thinks the skeptic, we should actually accept this illusion. For even the merely *apparent* prayer can always be a pretty good exercise in meditation. It can give us a certain inner concentration to counteract the ever-present centrifugal forces of dispersion and confusion in life. Yet the thinking man will never be able to overlook the fact that he is only acting "as if" he were speaking to God, and that he can accept this "as if" because it is a productive sort of self-delusion.

But there are moments when not only the skeptic, but even the *Christian* discovers that he has certain reservations about prayer. Lord Melbourne articulated these reservations in his second question: "About *what* is it proper to pray?" Doesn't Jesus himself say, "Your Father in heaven knows what you need before you ask him"? But if God knows all that, what can be the sense of putting in requests through prayer and uttering all sorts of wishes and ideas? Wouldn't it be better to content oneself with saying simply, "Thy will be done," or even, "I'll take whatever he gives"? Even the Christian must always be surprised, hardly able to grasp the fact that God allows his own to influence him, so that we may speak with him as loving children do with their loving father.

If we wish to meditate a little on the mystery of prayer at this point, I must flash a red warning light right at the beginning:

A theoretical and external approach will never get at what really happens in prayer. The mere spectator or bystander remains hopelessly on the outside. In his novel, *Diary of a Country Priest*, George Bernanos said, "How can people who have hardly any experience of prayer speak about it so lightly?" A Trappist or a Carthusian monk would struggle for years to become a man of prayer, and then will any old dilettante come in and give a snap judgment over the concern of a whole lifetime? . . . Would anyone consider himself justified in handing down a judgment about music when he had only tickled the keys of a piano with his fingertips from time to time? And if a symphony by Beethoven or a Bach fugue leaves him cold, but when he looks at the people around him he sees the reflection of high rapture—whom will he mistrust if not himself?

In fact, have all the powerful men of prayer in the history of the kingdom of God—from Eli to Bodelschwingh[1]—been fools? Was it mere autosuggestion when Moses testified that God had spoken with him as with a friend? Is the joy that their hearts experienced in conversation with the object of their hope, with the heavenly Father, or the peace of an indescribable security which that joy brought nothing but their own happy state of mind which they have projected on a blank wall? Or, might it be that the rest of us with our silenced hearts and our lack of prayer are the failures and the cheated ones?

In my life I have spoken too many times with honest, fruitless seekers and have myself been stuck too deep in trouble not to listen to a very serious counterquestion at this point. This objection could run, "I myself cannot pray. But if I have formed a judgment about prayer I am not simply a blind man who has the audacity to talk about colors. For after all, I have had personal experiences with prayer. Unfortunately they were negative and somewhat bitter. Sometimes despair released an impulse prayer in me. When I was in prison camp the insane hunger-pains made me cry out for bread. When I was in the bomb shelters and the earth shook around us while incendiary fires broke out everywhere, a distress-filled cry, 'Lord, help me,' escaped my lips. Granted: I did get a couple of bread crusts afterward, and I finally got out of that subterranean dungeon alive. But once I was sated and safe again, the need for that cry of prayer was automatically silenced. It was dumb within me. And what seemed like a prayer in the moment of danger appears to me in retrospect to be simply the expression of panic. I simply couldn't bring it off anymore."

Who hasn't had a similar experience? And yet precisely this

1. Bodelschwingh was a hospital administrator who opposed Hitler's program of euthanasia [Trans.].

experience, if we think it through, can lead us to the peculiar mystery of prayer.

What really happens in me when I catch myself, someone who otherwise stands outside the orbit of prayer, suddenly establishing a connection with God through an impulse prayer in a time of need? If we are honest, we must admit that we are not concerned about seeking the Father's hand so that we can be sheltered in the lee of his peace from the storms that rage around us. We really aren't addressing the *Father* when we do that, but only our growling stomachs or the bombs which threaten us, or the cancer we fear in our bodies. Once the bread is available and we are again filled, once the tumor has been taken out and our good health has returned, then the question of prayer is suddenly of no interest to us. It goes back to sleep. Obviously it was not the Spirit of God that enabled us to cry "Abba, dear Father"; it was only our nerves which had conjured up the bread and the bombs and the tumor as false gods. Our nerves had required us to perform nothing less than a little magical incantation in the form of an impulse prayer.

Whoever is determined to pray (really "pray"), however, must reach for the *hand* of God and not for the *pennies* in his hand. Whoever is solely interested in the pennies has no interest in the hand after he has received his reward. For to him the hand was only the means to an end, giving him his small change or pulling him through a danger. Afterward he pushed the hand away. It is of no more use; it has done its duty and can withdraw.

Do we understand, therefore, that a prayer can be nothing less than blasphemy? What is it but blasphemy when God is merely my means to an end? That takes its toll. If we turn God into a puppet of our desires (even when that happens by the pious route of prayer) then he shuts up his heaven and we find ourselves thrown back into the silence of our unredeemed life. Perhaps we say when it grows so still around us, "God is silent," or even "God isn't there." He really *isn't* there anymore, that's true. He really isn't there—not at all because he doesn't exist, but, as Léon Bloy once said, because he "withdrew" (*Dieu se retire*). Paul also makes suggestions that point in the same direc-

93

tion. For a short-lived success, perhaps because our nerves played tricks on us, we pushed away the hand of God's blessing and grabbed for the pennies that thereby fell from it.

I once heard of a child who was raising a frightful cry because he had shoved his hand into the opening of a very expensive Chinese vase and then he couldn't pull it out again. Parents and neighbors tugged with might and main on the child's arm, with the poor little creature howling out loud all the while. Finally there was nothing left to do but to break the beautiful, expensive vase. And then as the mournful heap of shards lay there, it became clear why the child had been so hopelessly stuck. His little fist grasped a paltry penny which he had spied in the bottom of the vase and which he, in his childish ignorance, would not let go.

We human beings constantly deal with God exactly like that foolish child. For the sake of a wretched penny in our grasp that we want to keep, the valuable container of our sonship with God is smashed. If we only *wanted* this highest good, to be God's children, seriously and with all our power, then we would *also* receive the penny, the healing, the protection in need, and everything else along with it. In any case, the one who is really cheated is the person who only prays when he is in need and who lets God be a good man the rest of the time. For he pays too high a price. He sacrifices the valuable vase for the penny of a moment's help.

That, by the way, was precisely what pained Jesus after the miraculous feeding in the wilderness when he said to the people, "You seek me, not because you saw signs, but because you ate your fill of the loaves" (John 6:26). He had miraculously fed the multitude so that they would perceive the true bread from heaven behind that event, so that they would learn to know the fatherly hand which led them and cared for them—that hand from which tenderness and mercy flow. To the multitude, however, that event remained opaque. It did not become "transparent" for them. So they overlooked the Father's hand and yearned only for the "five loaves and the two fish." Had they glimpsed the giver behind the gift and the Savior behind the bread, *this* experience would have stayed with them and accompanied them on through their life. Then they would have known from then on: we may drag ourselves along the thirsty miles in the desert, but our Father is with us. He can provide oases with fresh water for us. And even when we must go on and thirst again, he can embrace us with his peace, so that the thirst cannot bother us. Yet they declined this gift which he offered them in the miracle. Once their cry for bread was answered, they did not say, "To God alone be the glory," or "Glory be to God in the highest"; instead, they rubbed their overstuffed stomachs and murmured a satisfied "What a meal!" Then they got up to play and forgot the whole thing.

Our text discusses the question of what is involved in real, genuine prayer. It illustrates the idea with the image of a son who asks his father for something. That is the presupposition of prayer: that we are dealing with our *Father* and that we are his children. Without this presupposition nothing of it makes any sense. And since Jesus Christ shows us the Father, since in him this Father steps to our side and is *here*, Jesus is also involved in our prayer, so we pray "in his name."

And now we are told in no uncertain terms—it sounds almost arbitrary and unconditional—"Pray! It will be given to you. Seek! You will find." Certainly no earthly father will give his child a stone when he asks for a piece of bread. How much less would your heavenly Father do such a thing!

O.K.—does he really avoid doing it?

How often have we begged for something and *not* gotten it? Aren't there countless tombstones of unanswered prayers along the path of our life? Don't we all know of bitter disappointments and moments when there was neither speech nor answer as we fervently prayed, so that we remained in emptiness, disappointed and alone?

In order to find an answer to these pressing questions, we must ponder the very fine distinction between "asking" and "wishing." There certainly are such things as vain wishes, but in no case does one ask in vain. Many of our pious-sounding prayers are nothing more than sentimental wishes. But Jesus never promised the Holy Ghost to those who wished for something; the promise was to those who prayed earnestly and sought purposefully. When someone says, "Wouldn't it be nice if God's grace and truth reigned in my heart or if he presented me with a car or a new house," that is no prayer; it is pious slop. The person who "prays" does not address a wish to an unknown; he applies to a specific address and knocks on one certain door.

One can observe that precision in the traditional church prayers. When I was a young man I never understood properly why they always used such longwinded and ceremonious addresses: "Lord our God," "dear heavenly Father," and then came a relative clause "thou that art this and that and doest thus and so." And finally it was emphasized that he was the Father of our Lord Jesus Christ—and only after all that the things we wanted from him came out in a gradual and somewhat ceremonious way: Peace on earth, favorable weather, comfort for the lonely, and much more. But the ceremonious and formal-sounding address took nearly all your breath, so that you were almost exhausted by the time you reached the petitions themselves.

Gradually it became clear to me what those old experienced men of prayer were doing when they put such ceremonious addresses at the beginning: they wanted first and foremost to seek the face of God. They wanted to get the exact address. And if they wanted to "cast all their care upon him," they didn't start before they had pinpointed the *goal* of their casting. For they knew that the most important part of prayer is to come into the presence of God, because we have the promise that we will be accepted and heard. I have this certainty, however, only when I have aimed very precisely and when I am certain that it is God himself who gives me the power to come before him in that way. I also know that I may call upon my brother Jesus Christ to join hands with me and appear with me before my Father.

I said a moment ago that, seen in this way, there was no such thing as an unfulfilled prayer. I would like to prove that by a brief consideration of the question.

Naturally I have had the experience common to every other person who prays—God has *not* given me exactly what I asked for from him. But Jesus didn't say at all (if one examines it carefully!) that those who asked their Father for bread would, under all circumstances, receive that bread. He says only that under no circumstances would they receive a stone. He wants to tell me that in no case will the Father leave me in the lurch. Maybe I have prayed to God for something quite foolish. Maybe I looked for a raise, while God knew better than I that I needed modesty and a curb for my ambition. But how comforting, how beautiful it is, that I may also ask for such foolish things, that I can be myself, and that I don't have to talk like a precocious child with stilted words that are much more mature and wise than I myself.

I simply cannot speak "intelligently" with my heavenly Father. There is a very profound reason for that. For in order to bring a "legitimate" request that would stand up under God's scrutiny, I would have to be in a position to second-guess the Lord of history. I would need to possess something of that wisdom which enables him to guide events and to make even the "evil powers" of men serve his own ends. A hymn was once sung about Napoleon's army, which had perished in the expanses of wintry Russia:

> Horse and rider in that hour,
> Were stricken by the Lord's great power.

Thus the hymn implied a judgment by God, and many prayers by people living then tended in the same direction. But couldn't a Frenchman be of the opinion that this defeat was not a judgment against Napoleon, but rather a judgment against Europe, since it would now have to go without Napoleon's organizational genius? In the defeat of Napoleon, therefore, was a scourge broken as much as a savior, a representative of law and order, overthrown?

I would just about have to be a super philosopher, or better yet a prophet, to understand the whole picture of God's world rule so that I could ask God for the really "right" and "necessary" things. If I want to pray "correctly" and conform my requests to the will of God, that is what it will take. Yet God doesn't require that of me at all. I can say how I see the future frankly, freely, and openly; I can tell how I would like things to turn out and I may fit my requests to these somewhat childish (if measured by the standards of eternity) ideas.

Since I know, however, how immature this request of mine is, and how it therefore cannot be fulfilled by him who knows my actual need much better than I do, when I am done I should draw a thick line under my petition and say, "Not my will, but thine be done." Of course I know *to whom* I say that and to whose hands I thereby entrust myself; I realize that my Father knows what I need before I ask him, that he gives me what I need, and that he lets me recognize his gift, his answer, and his fulfillment in what at first may have seemed a strange answer or even no answer at all.

The phrase, "Thy will be done," however, can be said in a totally untrusting and blasphemous manner.

This "surrender to God's will" becomes blasphemous when we use it to avoid our own concern and action, saying instead, "As men we have no responsibility—neither for calling out the national guard nor for ending the war, neither for the race problems nor for the issue of labor's participation in industrial management. If I simply hand the matter over to God in trust, he will fix it." That is all pure blasphemy. Even though it sounds pious, on the other hand, a person who prays in earnest and struggles with God makes a peculiar discovery.

He discovers that the things *themselves* become important to him and that they fill him with practical thoughts and make him wrestle for the right action and the practicable solution. The things I consider important enough to bring to God can certainly not remain matters of indifference to me. When I ask God's involvement, I *myself* must be involved. If I wrestle with God in prayer over the rescue of a person, then I become profoundly concerned about this person myself. Thus prayer is at the same time an initiation into responsible action and some hard thinking.

I can also misuse the petition, "Thy will be done," in still another blasphemous way. That happens when I am basically a believer in fate and tell myself, "What will be, will be. There-

fore let God do what he will. His will be done; his will roll on!"
It is precisely at this point that everything depends on *to whom*
I say, "Thy will be done." Do I say it to *fate* and thus submit
myself to be driven by outside forces; or do I say it to my
Father with the intention of expressing this: "Now make out of
my dull prayer whatever will be useful to your decree. I *must*
speak with you, Lord, even if what I say is foolish, because I
love you and cannot keep silent since you have won my heart.
I thank you that I may come to you with my needs and suggestions and that you even *expect* me to pour out my heart to
you. Now transform my foolish prayer into whatever will best
serve my neighbor and me—you alone know what that is. And
if you wish to take from me the *one* person concerning whose life
I prayed to you, grant that I may accept even the loneliness
as your gift and that I may discover in it the traces of your
blessing."

If I wanted to tell what I think is the greatest thing we can
learn about prayer from the Bible, then I would say that the
greatest is that we come into the presence of our Father through
the conversation of prayer, that we taste his peace in the midst
of all unrest, and that we attain a place to stand against everything that presses in upon us and threatens to get the best of us.

When God lets our prayer succeed and his face shines upon
us, by the time we come to the "Amen" we have sometimes
forgotten the wish that originally drove us to pray. All at once
it has become unimportant because we are overwhelmed to
discover that in *any* case we will receive whatever will serve us
best.

So it is not important whether or not misfortune befalls us,
but whether we know the place of refuge and the space under
the shadow of his wings (Ps. 57:1). It is not important whether
we think we are being persecuted or that everyone is against
us, but only whether the Head is our friend and we are beloved
by God.

The tower beams of this church may have collapsed and
burned from incendiary bombing during the war, but afterward
an artist came who took a badly scarred and charred beam and
carved out an angel with a comforting and unspeakably

99

peaceful face. God, too, is an artist who, despite our pleas, allows much that we hold dear in this life to shatter. For his thoughts are higher than our thoughts. He is still able to take the rubble of our life and to build bridges and stepping-stones out of them, by which he leads us over all abysses. And no depth may swallow us.

> Since neither end nor limit
> May be found in God's love,
> I lift my hands, then,
> Father, to thee, as thy child;
> I ask that thou wouldst give me grace,
> With all my might,
> To embrace you day and night
> Throughout my whole life here
> Until, after this time is over,
> I praise and love you in eternity.
> > Amen.

48261

7. WHAT HAS GOD TO DO WITH THE MEANING OF LIFE?

And as he was setting out on his journey, a man ran up and knelt before him, and asked him, "Good Teacher, what must I do to inherit eternal life?"

And Jesus said to him, "Why do you call me good? No one is good but God alone. You know the commandments: 'Do not kill, Do not commit adultery, Do not steal, Do not bear false witness, Do not defraud, Honor your father and mother.'"

And he said to him, "Teacher, all these I have observed from my youth."

And Jesus looking upon him loved him, and said to him, "You lack one thing; go, sell what you have, and give to the poor, and you will have treasure in heaven; and come, follow me."

At that saying his countenance fell, and he went away sorrowful; for he had great possessions.

And Jesus looked around and said to his disciples, "How hard it will be for those who have riches to enter the kingdom of God!"

And the disciples were amazed at his words. But Jesus said to them again, "Children, how hard it is to enter the kingdom of God! It is easier for a camel to go through the eye of a needle than for a rich man to enter the kingdom of God."

And they were exceedingly astonished, and said to him, "Then who can be saved?"

Jesus looked at them and said, "With men it is impossible, but not with God; for all things are possible with God."

Mark 10:17–27

How does it happen that the question about eternal life, about the essentials, arises in a person? It may be some young person (as in this story) who is suddenly moved by this question. It doesn't always come up in such a way that the key words "eternal life" are used. Perhaps a completely different code is used to encipher the question.

For example, the young man could ask, "Who does the right thing with his life: Albert Schweitzer, who gives up a great academic career, who is not interested in a dream house, but goes into the African bush instead to busy himself with the un-appetizing illnesses of the natives—*or* the successful business man with his Mercedes and his mosaic tile swimming pool? What makes the difference? Does it come from a person losing himself in the service he performs—*or* does it come from prestige, career, success, and ultimately from appearing on the cover of a news magazine? What is the essential point around which all else revolves?"

In asking that question, the young man—more implicitly than explicitly—has posed the question of eternal life.

But an old man asks this question too. Perhaps he has just retired. His place at the office has been filled by someone else. No one waits for him any more. No one minds if he sleeps until noon. When he drops in at the office his old co-workers are nice to him, but he notices that he is only in the way. They have other things to attend to. And then the old man asks himself, "What have I really lived for? Have I brought anything essential into my barns to nourish me and fill me in these days? Or did I fool myself in thinking that everything depended on how much work I did, and am I now forsaken and superfluous, now that I only vegetate and am able to do *nothing*?" In suffering this shock of uselessness, the old man also, although implicitly and not explicitly, was posing the question about eternal life: the question of what really makes the difference in life and of what doesn't fade away when my productive functions in society cease.

What is the real goal of my life? That is the question we cannot dodge.

Of course it *is* possible to ignore the question. What a rush we all are in! I am overjoyed if I can get today's work finished and off my desk. I have no time to think about that distant future, that final goal, at which all this shall one day end. That is a luxury of the lazy, or a hobby for contemplative minds. And yet Albert Einstein once said, "We live in a time of perfect means and confused ends." We have refrigerators and television sets; we have social programs that make life easier and safer. Yet they are all means to make life more worth living. But what do we do with all those things? How perfectly and cleverly a television set or a sound movie camera operates! But what Hee-Haw-Hillbilly-Laugh-In soap operas do these clever devices help to produce! Does it really require that immense technical outlay to utter such breathtaking banalities? Is this inane babbling the goal toward which our technical perfection leads? What have we accomplished by that? What is our real goal?

Doesn't this hollowness, our lack of a goal and our inability to discover the meaning of life in all our achievements, lead to boredom? The comfort of our world is only attractive at first sight. The next moment we take it for granted and it becomes insipid. The fact that adolescents provide themselves with some bizarre excitement is only a symptom of this boredom.

But even the pious church-going Christian can pose this question about eternal life. The young man in our story could be called an officer of his church, one of the active laymen. He was a leader, denominationally speaking. It can happen that even such a man suddenly must ask, "Where in all the dogmas and doctrines can I find anything throbbing with life? Where can I find something to overpower me and conquer the gloom that comes over me from time to time? How many times in my life have I heard the Christmas message, 'I bring you good tidings of great joy!' I know those words inside and out. And yet so far they have never swept me along and lifted me out of my seat. They haven't made me really joyous and warm so far. How often at the Lord's Supper have I heard, 'Thy sins are forgiven thee.' I have taken it seriously and have wanted to make a new start. But the next day the old routine set in and I once again did what I had bitterly lamented at the altar. Where, then, is that famous life from God that is supposed to sweep you up and reshape you? Maybe I don't care that much about 'Truth.' Apparently I'm not that intellectual and 'highbrow.' But *life* means much to me; I'm interested in a reality which I feel, before which I must bow, and which can make clear to me in a flash: *That* is it; *that* is what matters! I am caught in religious routine and utter the empty words of a Christian vocabulary. I ought not to say—the church-going Christian may think—but I'm sick and tired of it."

This, then, is the frame of mind—and we all share it—in which this young man comes to Jesus. This question can be more important and more vital to a person than the problem of unpaid bills or a stomach that acts up after a big meal. And that is the case with this young man as he runs up and kneels in front of Jesus.

One must have this scene clearly in mind if one is to gauge its significance: People press in upon Jesus from every side. Most of them are simple people. It is already a bit awkward when a man in well-pressed, aristocratic clothes turns up in the midst of this somewhat ordinary multitude. But he doesn't just turn up, he kneels in front of Jesus. That causes a sensation. A man doesn't decide to do something like that unless it is a matter of life and death. A person has to be brimming over with something not to care about the impression he makes on other people or about making a fool of himself. (We saw how Zacchaeus, the tax collector, was similarly above his compromising situation.) A comparable situation might arise today during a rush for tickets to a Super Bowl game, when a fan is so obsessed with the idea that he has to see the game that he pushes up to the window without giving a thought to the fact that the other people in line may think he is crazy.

Thus what is going on around him or who is there doesn't make a bit of difference to the rich young man. As far as he is concerned there is only this *one* man Jesus and this *one* question that has become his destiny. Now what happens?

We are to assume that both Jesus and his disciples rejoiced. At last a man from the power structure and not merely the usual little people! At last someone who doesn't want money or a little casual discussion, or someone with all the bodily aches and pains who was simply looking for the miracle doctor. *Finally, finally a man with a basic question.*

How many counselors, their consultation rooms filled by simple people with everyday routine problems, wish passionately that just *once* in the week someone—only one!—came to them with a question of that nature, driven by the great unrest about what is essential.

"Good master," says the man, "what must I do to attain

eternal life?" "Tell me something about the meaning of my life, for I have lost it, and tell me whatever you want me to do. I will bear any burden, even an additional commandment or two for the elite (noblesse oblige!), if I only have the feeling that I am in harmony with myself and my destiny. I can't stand living any more if I have no theme to my life. I am caught in meaninglessness. And please don't let outward appearances deceive you into thinking that all is well .with me. Good master—please!" Isn't Jesus now supposed to raise him from the ground and tell him, "Thank you for coming to me with this question. I am pleased to encounter a seeking man like you"? But Jesus' reaction is strangely different from what we expected. He has nothing but a dash of cold water for this young seeker. He rejects—did he really have to start off that way?—being called "good master." "No one is good—only God alone."

Why does Jesus say that? Why does he say it at this particular time? Obviously because the rich young man sees Jesus as some sort of *teacher* who has certain patent recipes at his disposal which can help the man out of his life's uncertainties. The young man seems to think that one can bypass God in finding a solution to these problems. Jesus is a sort of "Dear Abby" for him. If you look at the questions readers send in to the problem columns of our newspapers you will notice that they are all pitched in the same key: I suffer from loneliness. How can I find contacts for lively companionship? My husband has left me and has gone away. How can I save my marriage? No one dances with me, how can I make myself attractive?

Dear Abby and her colleagues often provide very helpful suggestions to these questions. They give sound advice about what could be changed, and one even feels they have a warm-hearted desire to help. But a soul-doctor of that sort would obviously be over his head if someone demanded more of him than a little fiddling with the symptoms—for example, if one expected a cure of the basic problems. Nevertheless, good advice and a little adjustment of life-style are not to be sneezed at.

Jesus, however, proceeds entirely differently with this young man. He immediately rejects the level on which "good advice" is usually offered. When a person places himself in Jesus' care, he lays a sharp axe to his own roots; "If you just want a prescription for your life's problems from me," he tells the young man who kneels before him and watches him with burning expectation, "then you've come to me on false grounds. Therefore please don't say 'good master' or 'distinguished doctor' to me, as though I possessed patented rules which could help you get control of your life. Your life's problems cannot be solved as long as you push on past the *one* and *decisive* question: How you stand with God. In him alone is the good that you seek; he is the goal you are pursuing and the meaning you crave. No one is good—only God alone."

Perhaps one or another of us finds it peculiar that, in this case, God appears not only in the area of the pious inner life, but that he occurs as a very real and decisive factor in everything that is uncontrolled, questionable, and anxiety-producing in our life: that God is to be involved with our marriage, with our professional life, with our loneliness, and with our state of anxiety. In order to understand our story, we need to ponder this question for a moment.

Why is it that I feel lonesome and misunderstood? As a rule I just don't let this feeling surface. There is the TV in the evening, and tomorrow I have a party. Naturally I feel very superficial because of that, as though I were living on the edge of my own being, but nevertheless, it helps me forget for a while. Yet once in a while the set doesn't work, or I have a cold and have to stay home. Then I cannot avoid being alone. Then I don't know what to do with myself. The emptiness of my life gets on my nerves and puts me in a pensive mood. Who actually stands by me then? Who would really be there if I had a bad day? Would there really be an emptiness, an unfilled place, if I disappeared? Maybe that is when, as someone recently recounted to me, I dial the time service on the telephone simply to hear a human voice.

How different it would be if I could pray, so that a "thou" were there who said to me, "Fear not," or "I have called you by your name, you are mine," or "Peace be with you." Could my loneliness have something to do with the fact that I have deserted God? Wouldn't my marriage and my friendships that

I don't have but want to make so badly be different if I were calmer, if I were more content with myself, if I were less suspicious and uptight—in short, if I lived out of the peace of God and radiated the liberation of a person who knew that God watched over him and gave him a clear conscience? Wouldn't everything really appear in a different light if *this* question, this question about *God*, were settled for me?

That is the reason for the remarkably unfriendly gesture with which Jesus meets the overwrought young man's problems: "I am no answer man, if you please. I have no universal prescriptions for life. You have to build your life over from the ground up. You must begin by asking who and what God is to mean to you before I can help you."

Now we seem to be only one single step away from a lively religious discussion, one of those conversations which always end, like most discussions of this sort, in a draw. Yet Jesus does not discuss; he makes stern and most compelling claims. To get to deal with God is not a pious feeling; it means to be faced with his commandments. It means to enter the sphere of an unconditional obligation. Thus Jesus goes through the commandments: You shall not kill, you shall not commit adultery, etc. "Take God seriously," he is saying, "that's all. In performing this experiment you will find the 'meaning' for yourself and approach eternal life."

The rich young man is shocked indeed by this answer. "*I* am grappling with the ultimate things in life and he recites the catechism to me like a kindergarten teacher. He gives me a bottle when I crave bread. I've got *problems*, Jesus of Nazareth, *problems*. But you put me in kindergarten."

The young man only *thinks* all that; he doesn't say it. He controls himself sufficiently to content himself with a brief answer that barely indicates his disappointment: "I have kept all of them from my youth; I *have* taken God seriously, believe me. And nevertheless I have come to a point where I no longer know what to do. All of that has *not* brought me peace. If I thought that was the way to settle things with God, I surely wouldn't be standing here!"

This rich man is certainly *more* than a person with "religious

interests," more than a mere seeker who, like Faust, feels sure
that he will not find anything ultimately binding, but remains
caught up in spiritual adventuring, where he can play around
without obligation. No, this man has been stern with himself.
He has not merely tried a little philosophy of religion and played
with the God question; he has taken the issue of God so seriously that he declares his bankruptcy here in front of strangers
and semipublicly. The embarrassing situation he has gotten
himself into doesn't bother him at all.

But the question now is: Doesn't this man live in a remarkable self-deception? Is it ever possible to say so simply, "I have
kept the commandments of God"?

Outwardly, on the level of external deeds it may be possible.
He probably had not committed flagrant adultery and had not
stolen any silver spoons. But hadn't he ever observed what went
on *behind* the scenes of his outwardly proper acts: How he had
hated and killed his brother in his thoughts even if he outwardly
gave him a helping hand? And how he looked at a woman with
desire, committing adultery in his heart? How in foolish
attacks of envy—of course outwardly nothing was noticeable—
he robbed his neighbor of everything the man had and owned,
things the neighbor himself craved? Adalbert Stifter said in his
novel *Confidence*, "Each of us has a tigerlike quality, and no one
knows what atrocity he would be capable of in a fit of rage,
when all the inhibitions disappeared." Had the rich young man
never considered what thus, unnoticed by men's eyes, but
observed by God, churned and raged in his heart, and how
behind the scenes he sabotaged God's commandments piece by
piece and one after the other? Isn't he merely playing around
with the God question? Doesn't he have a blind spot that
enables him grandly to ignore all those shortcomings and to
say with the ring of conviction, "I have kept all the commandments from my youth. I have always taken God seriously"?

Certainly that is the sore spot in his life. But the astonishing
thing is that Jesus doesn't dig into what this man has done
wrong or where he has gone astray. Rather the story says
simply, before the conversation continued, "And Jesus, looking
upon him, loved him." I find that to be one of the most com-

forting places in the whole New Testament. Jesus does not love me just when I do something right, when I am therefore perfect and fit. Long before I get to that point, and even when I don't make it, I am *already* beloved. He always has the initiative.

Perhaps I am a young man who as yet hasn't gotten started with him. I have only a great hunger and thirst and many questions on my heart. And since I am still quite helpless, I poke around in Nietzsche, let a few verses by Gottfried Benn dissolve on my tongue, nibble a bit on Sartre, and even leaf through a few pages—why not?—of the Bible. Let's see what speaks to me there; let's see if anything there grips me! In my helplessness, what else can I do than let everything pass in review? And as I do that—perhaps with a cigarette, lying on the rug or curled up on the couch—while everything is still very vague and unclear, there stands Jesus before me, looking at me with affection. Everything that I do—even when it is wrong and I keep on pressing the wrong buttons—everything is included, embraced, and borne by that love. I cannot leave the force-field of that loving glance.

We must remember that, keeping it in mind when Jesus switches to the attack a moment later. For that is what he does. We must put up with the fact that Jesus can also be hard, that he gives us opposition; and that he is not at all like the feminine, coiffeured male fitted out with a halo that popular Christian art has made him. But when he thus leads the attack against the rich young man, we must watch it against the background of this *other* word: "Jesus, looking at him, loved him." The attack itself consists of one single sentence: "One thing you yet lack for perfection; go and sell all that you have. Give what you make by doing that to those who have nothing. Thus you will receive a treasure which is prepared for you in heaven. And then come, join my followers."

It is remarkable that for Jesus there is always one crucial thing: "One thing is needful"; "One thing you lack." Each one of us could count up on his fingers a list of who knows how many items that he still needs in order to make his joy complete. Jesus, however, is the great simplifier. For him, everything that we have to hope and fear reduces itself to the figure "one." Basically there is only *one* problem in my life, only *one* sore spot, only *one* possibility of healing. Everything else arranges itself according to how I start off with this one and primary element.

Thus he says to the rich young man, "You lack one thing." But what a striking thing to point out as lacking! "Sell all you have!" The young man was not prepared for that. No one ought to expect such tomfoolery from him. That was the second dash of cold water he had received. He belonged to the intelligentsia, so he immediately began to calculate: "What would we come to if such a clearance sale were necessary for perfection? Isn't that nonsense? If I sold everything to become perfect, then wouldn't I make the others whom I urged to buy from me imperfect? Then my partner in the sale will have to bear the moral expenses of my ennoblement! That doesn't make sense!" "Or," he calculates further, "if everyone were to sell all they had, who would be left to buy? What kind of crazy economic system would we have then? That is unrealistic, Jesus of Nazareth, you can't expect any responsible person with good sense to do that!"

So the young man gets up disappointed, confused, and discouraged. How he had trusted this man and how serious he had been! In addition to the Ten Commandments which he had observed from his youth, he was ready to add an eleventh and twelfth commandment with even more difficult ethical training rules. He was ready cheerfully to pray for hours in a darkened room or to introduce two fast days in the week if that would have brought him closer to eternal life. "O yes," he thinks, "I was determined to go to any extremes. Instead of that, he comes out with this nonsense, to take away from me in the name of God all that the blessing of God had brought me. Like a mixed-up sectarian, he tries to destroy the order in life."

Hasn't this man deluded himself a second time? Won't he listen and understand what Jesus is saying to him in the code-language of that remarkable challenge? What, then, *did* Jesus want to tell him? Apparently he meant this: No doubt, dear friend, that you want to take God seriously and that you have tried hard. Precisely on account of that I now ask you if you have taken God *really* and *radically* seriously. Aren't you actually concerned about "religion," since you seek inner peace? Or since life seems hollow and empty to you, haven't you decided to try an experiment on that point? Or haven't you noticed that a reputation as a pious man could bring social advantages and that you would thus further increase the prestige to which your possessions have already helped you? Wasn't God merely a means to an end for you (in the way we today like to use him in order to oppose a Christian ideology to the Eastern menace, or to shore up the foundations of the Christian West)? Haven't you tried to fit religion into your life with this in view? Very earnestly, very decently, quite certainly. But has God ever meant more to you than a pious "extra" in life, more than a final polish for your standard of living, more than a pious nicety? "Try for once," Jesus tells him, "to test out the priorities. Are you ready to give up everything for God? Only if you could do that would it be shown that he is your one and only concern, that you trust him *completely* and that you take him seriously *without reservation.*"

Thus in that remarkable challenge of Jesus to sell all he had lies a challenge to an experiment: "Put everything you treasure and value in your life in the left pan of the scales. In that pan goes all that pertains to your life-style on which you depend (and I have nothing at all against that!); in addition, put your friendships, your social standing, and your talents there. And then put the weight that *God* has in your life in the right-hand pan. Then watch and see which side of the scale sinks." That is the most serious test; that is the fatal experiment. For then it will become clear that the pan which contains all in life that is near and dear to me sinks, having the greater weight, and God is taken more lightly.

Then the young man stood up sadly and went away disappointed "for he was very rich." He was a gifted man, and the left-hand pan in his life was very heavy. He wanted religion to be an extra aroma; he wanted to add the inner possession of breadth and depth of soul to all the outward possessions of his already rich life. Therefore down deep he was not looking for eternal life; he sought God as an elixir of life that would shake him loose from the boredom of the wealthy and give him some inner excitement. For him God was to be a final, crowning touch on life; he was to be the means to an end in life, but not to be that life himself.

But God will not sell himself for that price. One cannot speak of God to a person who has not asked himself the hard "all or nothing" question. Therefore the rich and gifted are perhaps the most endangered. A fully loaded camel cannot get through the needle's eye of a city gate. Sometimes a poor and unendowed man has it easier; all he has to do is hold up the hand God has given him. Or a child has it easier, because it has nothing itself and makes no claims.

"Then who can be saved?" ask the shaken disciples. Aren't we all, in one way or another, rich men—that is, people that have something in their lives of which they are proud and on which they have set their hearts? Therefore don't I myself stand in the balance-pan when I want to reach God—and not only with my darker instincts and normal qualms, but also with the very best in my life: my talents, my mental stature, and the core of interests on which all my choices depend?

Yes, that's the way it is; in fact, this is the mystery of the kingdom of God. It is certainly also its greatness. Or isn't it great and exciting that at *this* entrance gate and at *this* needle's eye no one is greater than another; that here all are alike: People from whom God must take all of life's burdens *and* gifts so that they become children who can allow themselves to be given what they need?

When Jesus Christ hung on the cross, when he no longer had anyone or anything, when his disciples were scattered to the four winds and even his robe had fallen into the hands of the gambling and drinking soldiery, *then* he was nearest to his Father. Then there was nothing else that stood between him and his Father. And he bowed his head and committed himself to the eternal hands. Here he had *nothing* left, and therefore the Father could be *everything* to him. Everyone who wants to have eternal life must pass through this "death and resurrection."

We certainly can't do it ourselves. We are not able to pry open those fists of ours with which we hold on tightly to what is ours. "With men it is impossible." God knows, it *is* impossible. But with God all things are possible.

The rich young man wasn't able to do it either, and he went away sorrowful. We don't know what happened to him after that. Did the One who saw him and loved him one day catch up with him? Was his leaving perhaps a last attempt at flight which he later gave up?

However things may stand with me—whether I hope to find the solution to my questions from this Nazarene or whether I am disappointed and can only shake my head in amazement over a story such as this—of one thing I can rest assured: Jesus Christ has also seen me and loved me. Now I can go wherever I will. There is no place to which this love does not extend and there is no space which these arms do not encompass.

PART TWO:

How to Love Again

8. WHERE IS MY FELLOW MAN?

And behold, a lawyer stood up to put him to the test, saying, "Teacher, what shall I do to inherit eternal life?"

Jesus said to him, "What is written in the law? How do you read?"

And he answered, "You shall love the Lord your God with all your heart, and with all your soul, and with all your strength, and with all your mind; and your neighbor as yourself."

And he said to him, "You have answered right; do this, and you will live."

But he, desiring to justify himself, said to Jesus, "And who is my neighbor?"

Jesus replied, "A man was going down from Jerusalem to Jericho, and he fell among robbers, who stripped him and beat him, and departed, leaving him half-dead.

"Now by chance a priest was going down that road; and when he saw him he passed by on the other side.

"So likewise a Levite, when he came to the place and saw him, passed by on the other side.

"But a Samaritan, as he journeyed, came to where he was; and when he saw him, he had compassion, and went to him and bound up his wounds, pouring on oil and wine; then he set him on his own beast and brought him to an inn, and took care of him.

"And the next day he took out two denarii and gave them to the innkeeper, saying, 'Take care of him; and whatever more you spend, I will repay you when I come back.'

"Which of these three, do you think, proved neighbor to the man who fell among robbers?"

He said, "The one who showed mercy on him."

And Jesus said to him, "Go and do likewise."

Luke 10:25–37

At the center of this story that we all know so well stands the question of the lawyer, "Who is my neighbor?"

We often think that the questions of biblical times are obsolete. We need to reinterpret them in order to find the level at which they "speak" to us.

That is hardly the case with the question, "Who is my neighbor?"

We have immediate access to that one. It holds for establishment types and for members of the subculture; it holds for lawyers and for tax collectors; it holds for the people of ancient Israel and for men of the atomic age. Recently in his (anti-) novel *Borders*, Jürgen Becker has compressed this question into a neat formula: "You. And who is that?"

Today we cannot trace out the entire breadth of our test; we will have to content ourselves with this *one* question, because it is also our question: "You. And who is that?"

For the contemporary mind, to say that one shall love one's neighbor means that one should regard him in the same way that God himself does. Since God does not forget our neighbor, we are closest to God when we are close to our neighbor (and vice versa).

This commandment to love one's neighbor had turned into "flesh and blood" for the lawyer. Jesus' partner in conversation took for granted, just as we do today, that "mankind"—the law of humanity—had to be the highest standard by which to judge our actions. This principle has almost become a rhetorical cliché for public speakers. It has long been considered a self-evident principle. Every child knows it.

When Jesus gives the lawyer the simplest possible answer here, "Do this self-evident thing, take it seriously, and your life will fulfill itself"—the lawyer feels a little foolish, since he recognizes that he has let himself in for a compromising situation. Because by his question he had raised a fundamental problem, a problem that keeps both theologians and philosophers busy. He had asked about eternal life and about the basis, goal, and meaning of human existence. That was not only an elemental problem of life, it was at the same time a highly intellectual problem.

And now the question, instead of leading to the heights of speculation, is to be disposed of by an allusion to what is self-evident! Jesus' answer means simply, "You don't need any great *speculation* over the meaning of life; you just need to do the ordinary, everyday things; you need only be there when your fellow man is in difficulty, then you are already in accord with that meaning. Then you are not merely seeking that meaning; you are in the process of fulfilling it. For you will meet God himself in the imprisoned, the hungry, and the naked. When you are close to all of those, then you also dwell close to God, and you are in contact with the basic meaning and goal of your life." "As you did it to one of the least of these my brethren, you did it to me" is the way the Lord will express the same thing once again near the end of his life. "He who has the brother, has me": in this brief formula is conveyed the secret which contains the meaning of our life.

In its simplicity that is exactly as disconcerting as a statement which Gerhard Nebel once made as he described a nurse who had made a great impression on him because she was completely at peace with herself, well-adjusted, and radiating peace and protectiveness. He commented, "Self-sacrifice—the being-there-completely-for-the-neighbor—is the only effective remedy for neuroses and depressions." This prescription too is strikingly simple: The person who suffers from depression is led into endless acts of meditation and introspection. He broods over the things that frighten him, the emptiness that besets him, or future terrors that approach him. He never reaches the end, because such introspection follows a wrong path, a dead end. It revolves only about himself. He asks interminably, "Where do *I* find fulfillment? Where do *I* find my peace?" But as long as I make myself the theme and have the whole world revolve around my person, I will find no rest.

I remember a series of conversations in which a group of us discussed the various ages of man. One of this group mentioned an elderly lady of his acquaintance and said of her, "She has a good life; she doesn't need to worry about anyone anymore and she can do whatever her interests suggest." I was impertinent enough to ask, "Isn't that woman somewhat unusual? Is she really happy with her situation? Wouldn't it be frightful not to have to worry about anyone anymore?" And the answer came back, "Actually, that's the way it is. She feels she is anything but happy; she has a hundred aches and pains, and the doctor says that it is all psychological." She revolved

around herself, and her suffering was precisely the meaninglessness of her existence. The introspection and meditation on
what it was that oppressed her in ever-changing forms could
not alone break the spell of this circular movement; instead, it
only pulled her deeper into the whirlpool. The solution to her
life's question lay in her becoming "forgetful of self." "He lives
the best," Luther once said, "who does not live to himself; and
he lives the worst who lives to himself." Only the self-forgetful
person finds the peace of God and thus becomes secure within
the consciousness of those higher thoughts. The only place I
can reach God is where he chooses to be present: in my fellow
man, whom I help without thinking of myself, the fellow man
for whom I am available and whom I love. That is exactly what
Nebel meant by saying, "Self-sacrifice is the only remedy for
neuroses and depressions." The prescription appears to be that
simple when the issue is the ultimate questions of life.

The lawyer now finds himself in a painful position. The
dialogue which he began so spiritually ("What must I do to
inherit eternal life?") has ended with an indescribably simple,
in fact almost trivial, piece of advice. Is it right for God, as has
been said, to be stuck in the "details" of life, not to mention the
question of God in general being wrapped in the most everyday
terms? If that's where they are, then the solution to life's problems must be sought somewhere other than the places where
philosophers and debaters of world-views usually look. The
ultimate tormenting problems of life can only be laid to rest at
the point where we forget ourselves and our appointment books,
as the good Samaritan actually did. God himself will meet us
where we are present to our fellow man.

No wonder that the lawyer, faced with such simplicity,
endeavors to justify himself intellectually. In effect he gives
Jesus to understand, "If it were that simple, Jesus of Nazareth,
I could have figured it out for myself. I certainly would not
have needed any consultation on the case! Don't you see that a
new problem lurks in your simple prescription for life? You
have me simply recite the catechism like a schoolboy, repeating
the commandment to 'love your neighbor.' But this commandment, although it sounds simple, is full of mental traps: Tell

me, who *is* my neighbor? Is it my child or the person next door? Is it my colleague or my competitor? Is my neighbor the hungry man halfway around the world or the victim of war in Southeast Asia? Are the nearest and the farthest both included equally in the commandment? I am confused by the immense range of possibilities which this commandment places before me, Jesus of Nazareth! Ought we not set up priorities of need? Must there not be detailed guidelines for such a broadly worded commandment? All that must be cleared up first, Jesus of Nazareth—*first,* that is *before* I can begin to love my neighbor in a concrete way! You have dismissed my problems with simple phrases from the catechism. Now I am showing you by means of this one single question that you haven't helped matters at all, but that it is precisely here that the hardest problems begin. And this single question of mine is, 'Who *is* my neighbor? Where do I find him?' "

In this way the lawyer gained some time before he would have to take the commandment about loving one's neighbor seriously. He had built in the cushion of a discussion between himself and the hard necessity of the act. Perhaps the matter can be discussed to pieces, and thereby everyone avoids taking it seriously. That is probably his secret hope.

We know that the Lord blocked this way of escape and we know how he did it.

His story of the Good Samaritan ends with a disconcerting reversal of this question of who my neighbor is. The reversal runs as follows: Who among these three (priest, Levite, and Samaritan) had behaved as a neighbor? Who acted the part of a neighbor to the man who had fallen into the hands of robbers?

No other answer can be given to that question than the one the lawyer is forced to give: "The one who showed mercy is the one who behaved as a neighbor."

As a result, the decisive question is no longer, "And who is my neighbor?" but "To whom am *I* a neighbor; where am *I* required? Where is anyone pinning his hope on *me*—his hope that I have time for him, that he is of any concern to me, that I shake off what is repulsive in him, that behind his vanity and aggressiveness I see the emptiness and the despair which he has not been able to master?"

The question, "To whom am *I* a 'fellow man'?" or, in Luther's formulation, "To whom am I to be Christ?" is, in fact, an order to service which tolerates no further argument or debate; it immediately requisitions me. It defines *me* as the neighbor. The theoretical question, "And who is my neighbor?" leads me into endless reflection, so that it never need issue in any obligation or involvement. The question, "To whom am *I* a neighbor?" on the other hand, puts me on a crash program. Everyone is caught by the phrase the moment he says it. Only when I am clear that the question about who is my neighbor ends in this order to service and that it cannot lead to the diversionary tactic of endless discussion may I look more deeply into that question. And under the shield of such a warning we will now take a moment to do that.

It seems to me that the question of the lawyer concerning who my fellow man is and consequently how I can bring my love for the neighbor to that man has acquired new and special emphasis for our generation. For the sake of honesty we must inquire whether we can thus simply apply the parable of the Good Samaritan to our situation.

In some respects this story does in fact address us directly: The Levite and the lawyer make a wide detour around the poor guy who has nearly been killed. We don't need a commentary to tell us what that has to say to us. We know from our own lives that we overlook the unhappiness around us. If we were fully aware of all the things the people around us struggle with—in our family, in our office, in our place of work—and if we were fully aware of the cries of the hungry, the degraded, and the suffering in the whole world, it would almost overwhelm us. Therefore we repress it and act as if we didn't see it. During the Third Reich we closed our eyes and ears to the treatment of Jews and the rumors of concentration camps. For *if* we had seen and heard something, it would have led to the dangerous duty of protesting. We didn't want to subject ourselves, though, to these dangerous protests. Therefore, exactly like the priest and the Levite, we made a wide detour around that screaming injustice and acted as though we had not seen it. In fact, the parable's complaint against our lovelessness addresses us directly. Love not only makes us discover resources for help, it first makes us discover the need itself. It lets us *see* the misery of our fellow men. Before love sets our hands in motion it opens our eyes. And if we see nothing and hear nothing, so that we are surprised at a suicide or a nervous breakdown in our neighborhood, that is exactly the hypocrisy that the parable is talking about. It is not because we neither saw it nor knew of it that we neglected to come to the rescue in love. It is exactly the opposite: Because we had no love, we saw nothing and looked for nothing.

All of that, as we have said, touches us directly. We need no commentary and no tedious translation into our present situation.

Yet that is not true for all parts of our text. Doesn't it present us with a patriarchal, and therefore obsolete, world? If that is so, can we carry this parable over into our totally different situation without commentary?

In the text, two individuals meet on the "open road": the wounded man and the Samaritan. But where in our thoroughly organized society is there an open road left? Where is there an area that is not built up and that offers the space for a direct, person-to-person humanity? Don't we live in a world of administrative machinery? For every form of human misery there is some institutionalized remedy available: If a traffic accident occurs, there is the highway patrol or the ambulance; for fires there is the fire department; for material need the social agencies; for epileptics the hospital; for mentally retarded the special school; and for everyone the welfare state. Does the Samaritan's deed of a single individual have a chance in this sort of world? Is it relevant at all? Isn't the love of neighbor which he practiced bound up with an obsolete social order? That is the question.

There could be no more foolish reaction to this question and statement than to raise an anthem in praise of the good old days in which there were no large organizations and no welfare state, and where therefore free and spontaneous acts of help were possible man-to-man; while in our day, the depersonalizing machinery has pushed itself in between me and thee. It would be frightful if Jesus' parable did not lead us into involvement, as it intends to do, but led us astray into romantic praise of the good old days. Then where is my fellow man today, in this modern world of social machinery? How can we bring love to bear on an individual *today*? Only when we hear the message of Jesus in this new and changed situation do we take it seriously.

No less a thinker than Karl Marx has pointed out that poverty and mass misery are grounded in the social structure. The capitalistic order, he argues, lets the rich become richer and the poor become poorer. But if that is so—and men generally, whether they are Marxists or not, agree that there is at least some truth in it—then it is bound to have some influence on the way in which I step in to help and therefore on how I practice love toward my neighbor.

A bit of philanthropy, a bowl of soup, and a dip into the pocketbook for especially needy cases doesn't help here at all. On the contrary, philanthropy can, as is stated at one point in Thornton Wilder's novel *The Eighth Day*, be nothing but "a roadblock on the way to social righteousness." That is because such individual acts of charity may simply cloud the real need, treating the gaping, bleeding wounds of the social organism with what amount to skimpy bandages, and dealing with symptoms rather than causes.

Then where is my neighbor? That now becomes the real question.

Is this neighbor really only the man I meet accidentally and directly, as the Samaritan met him on that road to Jerusalem? Or could this neighbor possibly be represented by whole groups of people—by the group of pensioners, who thus far have shared only partially in the prosperity of our nation, or by the huge group of young people whose extravagance in music and dress usually gets all our attention, but whose loneliness is to be sought in totally different and deeper areas? Might this neighbor be caught in exploitive structures of society?

But if that is so, then this discovery clearly implies a task

124

for our love, or, more precisely, for the *shape* of our love. This love, in order to be effective, must be a planning, organizing, and in extreme cases (I think, for example, of South America) even a revolutionary love. In any case, it cannot limit itself merely to individual spontaneous acts of a so-called good heart. Love must desire a maximum effectiveness. But this maximum can only be achieved when love steps in systematically, and that requires planning.

I can imagine how a sequel to the parable of the Good Samaritan ought to be written in order to bring it up to date without losing a single speck of its basic thrust. This sequel could look somewhat like this:

The Good Samaritan certainly had an occupation of some sort. He wasn't a "Good Samaritan" by trade any more than Goethe was a "classic" by trade. So we may therefore feel free to imagine that he was the mayor of his village back home. Then how would he attend to the duty of loving his neighbor in his local political calling as impressively as he fulfilled it during his journey?

While sitting in his office, he would likely think over ways in which he could prevent similar assaults from occurring in his forests in the future. Thus his love is a precautionary love, seeking to prevent murder and assault ahead of time. It will become a preventative and planning and therefore to a certain degree a "political" love. Thus he may order the inhabitants of his village to comb the woods carefully for highwaymen. And then, if his people actually come up with some sinister and suspicious fellows, his love will have a further task. He will question those men about *why* and *how* they took this devious path of highway robbery. Perhaps he ascertains that they were needy and out of work, or that they had been badly treated by their employer, so that they ran away and now scrape along by robbery and attacking travelers. Or he uncovers the fact that they suffer under what today is called "environmental damage."

Then the Good Samaritan would once again obtain totally new tasks for his love. He would know that his love called him to combat the *causes* which led to that highway robbery.

125

Perhaps he would become active as a social reformer, or even a social revolutionary, in order to serve, to help, and to ward off future harm from his neighbor. Love also makes us inventive: It constantly develops new *methods* by which it can become effective; and it lays claim to our ideas and imagination so that we discover those methods. Love of our neighbor has as many forms as there are places and systems in which our neighbor can be concealed. We discover ever new dimensions in the parables of Jesus. Ever new surprises await us there. They are never too old and never out of date.

Naturally this short sequel to the parable of the Good Samaritan is fantasy; nevertheless it is an expository, interpretive fantasy that listens carefully to the sense of the parable. It thereby becomes clear to us that Jesus wants more than improvised ad hoc acts of charity from us; he wants foresighted love. Love can demand politically and socially effective action of me; it can require me to become involved with aid programs and with demands affecting the entire social structure. My neighbor is not just the individual "thou" whom I happen to encounter in my neighborhood or at my place of work. My neighbor is also the next generation which I must help (for *love*'s sake I must help) through the educational system so that they achieve goals worth living for. My neighbor can also be a group within society which I consider to be disadvantaged and with which I identify myself.

At the same time, however, the individual "thou" about whom the Good Samaritan was concerned retains his significance. Clearly institutions and orders cannot be converted. Only the individual person can do that. And this conversion evidences itself in my neighbor encountering me as that fellow man for whom Jesus Christ died; he was therefore purchased at a high price and is valuable in God's sight. Those who think only of world renewal and who seek to attain it through the perfection of social structures are indulging in utopian dreams; they strive for a world of dead apparatus without security. This world is depicted for us in the novel *Fox Fire* by Drieu la Rochelle. A suicide leaves a letter which reads in part, "I killed myself because I didn't love myself and I don't love you."

They all were nice to him; outwardly everything was in order. Perhaps the structure of his social environment also remained intact. But he lived in an oppressive void, in the chill of insecurity, that is, in a world without love. World renewal cannot begin by our dreaming of a utopian perfect world order, that's a fact; it begins with the discovery of the neighbor, with finding out that man is a being under God, whose destiny he was willing to let cost him something. Only from this mustard seed of a new relationship to the "thou" can the new tree of humanity grow, in which the birds of the air dwell and whose branches spread out over the earth (Mark 4:31–32).

With that we come to an important realization which may be reduced to two opposing thoughts:

First, a love that restricts itself merely to the individual sphere of "I and thou," becoming active only in occasional encounters with misery and need, robs Jesus' command of wide areas of application. It ignores the fact that Jesus has placed love in a very much broader perspective for us, that it also demands organization and planning on a grand scale so that our neighbor will be shielded from even the threat of harm in a more justly ordered society.

But a second approach is also true: Those who plan only for a utopian world of perfection—a world which is a paradise of righteousness and full stomachs, a world without problems in Asia and the Midcast—those who plan for such a world without having first discovered the mystery of the neighbor in the light of God's countenance will strive for a world in which only things and not men matter, a world of apparatus, a world-sabbath which does not exist for the sake of man (Mark 2:27) but only for its own sake.

Finally this text of Holy Scripture deals with none other than faith itself. I can only answer the question about who my neighbor is when I know who God is. For he alone allows the miracle to happen in which I become aware of my neighbor and discover in him the brother of my Lord, for whose sake he went to the cross. Only then does it become clear why the love of God and neighbor are bound together in one commandment.

When a person is granted the gift of saying, "My Lord and my God," he also sees the men who belong to God for whom the Father keeps a lookout—the prodigal sons: those who wander in a far country, those who are overcome with homesickness, those often bound and imprisoned, the hungering and the thirsting. He who can thus say, "My Lord and my God," is already led into that self-forgetfulness where he no longer revolves about his own ego, producing nothing but nightmares of emptiness and sadness. He is already reoriented toward others; there the face of God himself gazes upon him and leads him to complete fulfillment.

If I want to know what faith is—and how we long to have that experience!—then I am not to ask about the dogmas that this faith must energize; I am to keep a lookout to see what discoveries this faith makes, what new, breathtaking image of my fellow man is granted to it and what powers of love are released in it. "For the kingdom of God does not consist in talk but in power" (1 Cor. 4:20). And there, where the kingdom is present in power, where it is active in love, where it lets the scales fall from our eyes, where it stimulates our mind and imagination and makes our hands creative—there we are to seek faith. And we testify to faith by making ourselves instruments of its power. That is precisely what Thornton Wilder meant when he had one of his characters say, "Never ask a man what he believes. Watch what he uses. Faith is a dead word and brings death with it."

The Lord wants this parable to be a battlecry against dead faith and a summons to "use" true faith. Faith that is used, faith that is lived is the only kind of faith with the power to call the Lord into our midst with his overpowering presence. And when that happens, we discover our neighbor. There the miracle of love will transform me—and not only me, but the world as well.

9. HOW CAN I KEEP FROM BEING TORN UP INSIDE?

> But when the Pharisees heard that he had silenced the Sadducees, they came together. And one of them, a lawyer, asked him a question, to test him.
> "Teacher, which is the great commandment in the law?"
> And he said to him, "You shall love the Lord your God with all your heart, and with all your soul, and with all your mind. This is the great and first commandment. And a second is like it, You shall love your neighbor as yourself. On these two commandments depend all the law and the prophets."
>
> *Matthew 22:34–40*

The question about which commandment is greatest is here posed with a cunning, provocative goal in mind. It is intended to be a tactical maneuver. As always, the answer forces one person to put his foot in his mouth and gives his opponents ample opportunity to get their hooks in him. Since Jesus had just, to use Luther's graphic translation, "stopped the mouths" of the Sadducees, others were now eager to try another trick that would lure him out on thin ice.

It is not only a case, though, of the enemies of Jesus hatching an evil plot to trap him. Their question also suggests a serious motive. They are interested in what today is usually termed "involvement." They want a final and binding direction for life. They want to know what the unconditioned and absolutely obligatory thing in our life is. No one would dispute that that is a very serious question, raised by a sensitive conscience.

If, however, one asks this question about what is unconditionally binding, one is immediately faced with a dilemma. This occurs in two respects.

First, we must set up gradations in our catalogue of duties; we must decide on "degrees" of urgency. That is already clear in daily life. How many duties surround us; how many things ought we to look after? One of us is absorbed in his business, and he is worried about all the things he ought to do for his family. Which is more important, the expansion of my business, my official duties which depend completely on how much of myself I am willing to give, *or* my children to whom I should give my best instead of leaving them to themselves without any assistance? Won't there come a time, if I deny them my presence now, when I will receive a painful answer to that question? Won't they then have become alienated from me, adopting tastes and values which I consider shocking?

Since I thus continually face a conflict between duties of the most varied kind which sometimes tear me apart, must I not repeatedly ask which among all these demands is the *most* obligatory and holds the highest priority? Then look where I come out! We are *back* to the question of which is the greatest commandment.

Perhaps there is still another motive behind this question of the Pharisees. Perhaps they wish to learn of the highest value from which all others derive. This wish is similar to the longing for a universal formula which will explain all the phenomena of life and which will bring some sort of order, clarity, and outline to the confusing welter of occurrences. The fascination of world-views lies in the fact that they offer something of that explanation and ordering. For no matter how different they are—whether we think of the great system of Hegel or of Marxism—they always have an ultimate principle, an ultimate overarching theme to the world, a sort of "universal formula." Once a person has grasped *that*, he has the world itself by the tail. He can proceed to deduce how economic crises arise, how wars begin, and what level of value our personal life, love and marriage, and friendship and competition have in the total structure of the universe. It can be an indescribable relief and a downright joy to have the band that "holds the world together" within your control. No wonder that a universal formula of this sort, the knowledge of what is ultimately binding and meaning-producing, exerts a great fascination. No wonder that it gives impetus to life and releases immense energy for action.

And yet this human urge to find the one unconditioned demand leads into various blind alleys. Behind their effort to run the Lord into one of those blind alleys lie the two motives of the Pharisees: *first*, the desire to learn the ultimately binding principle and thus to be able to choose intelligently among demands, and *next*, the desire to capture the Master in the nets of unanswerable questions.

Why does it have to end in blind alleys? I wish to show that by an example.

There is a world-view, for instance, that traces back the wealth of all historical phenomena to specific economic structures. These structures form the material basis of all that happens and determine the nature of society. Now of course there can be no doubt that economic realities leave a decisive impression on human life and community. But *more* than that is asserted here; here the material underpinning of history is claimed to be the source of life in general, so that it comes close to being that universal formula we spoke of earlier. But if that is the case, then our life is significant only because it performs a function in the production process; in doing so it is important to the cohesion of society.

But, this is the question, can our human life with all its many dimensions be reduced to a piece in the social process? Where, in this point of view, is there room for the joy or unhappiness of our marriage, where is the love between parents and children, where is the faithfulness of friends, and where are all the questionable and pivotal emotions of the human heart— its loneliness and its hunger for community, its desire to destroy, its aggressive drives, or on the other hand, its longing to love and build up? What becomes of all that when we see the totality of our life determined by that questionable universal formula? That is why the poems of Yevtushenko could almost effect a revolution in Russia, evoking deep-seated responses within people's hearts simply because those poems sang of love and hate, of pride and loneliness. They dug up all the buried aspects of personal life that could no longer be brought into the narrow confines of that world-view.

The Pharisees hope to maneuver the Lord into a parallel

situation. They want to induce him to fish *one* normative and supreme commandment out of the wealth of God's commandments and the immense list of cultic prescriptions. Then he is to make that commandment into a sort of common denominator, really a type of "universal formula," that encompasses our whole religious and secular life.

Now if he plays that game and names a commandment that so completely dominates all the rest, it is inevitable that the moment I just spoke of will immediately arise. I refer to that moment when his questioner could ask, "And what about all the others? You have curtailed the will of God when you make everything depend on that one supreme commandment which you have chosen! In the most inadmissible way you have reduced the claims that God has upon us and trimmed them to fit your own ideas!"

Suppose Jesus had pointed to a ritual statute as being supreme, for example, the one that says the water of purification from the ashes of a red heifer has special expiatory power (Num. 19). Then his questioner would have said, "You narrow God's will to the cultic-sacral sphere. God, however, wants our *whole* life. He wants us to place house and home, food and drink, clothing and possessions, our whole worldly and communal existence, in the light of his countenance. Where is there room for that in the hierarchy of commandments which you have proposed here?" Perhaps they would remember Amos's words of rebuke and judgment, in which God shrugs off the bleating of pious hymns and the playing of psalms (Amos 5:23) when fellow men are forgotten in the pious religious services, when the poor are trampled in the dust and the disinherited are left to their misery (Amos 2:7). "In your concern for the commandment of God you have forgotten the service of mankind, Jesus of Nazareth!" That is surely the way their reproach would sound.

Suppose, however, that the Lord had answered instead, "The highest commandment is to love your fellow man." Then they probably would have argued the other way and said, "You are only concerned with social justice, and any respectable atheist could want the same thing. And if you pass that off as

132

the commandment of God, even though our unaided conscience knows that already without any transcendent assistance; then for you God is at best only another name for human brotherhood or for the unconditional nature, the authority, of this commandment. Where is *God* in this conception of yours, Jesus of Nazareth? You have stolen him away! You have dissolved him in brotherly love!" That is surely how they would have reacted to this second kind of answer.

Did the Lord allow himself to be checkmated in this way, or did he carefully avoid going into this question of the greatest commandment altogether?

Oh yes, he got into it, all right. But he did it with a disconcerting twist which stopped the mouths of the Pharisees as well. He did not pick out, as his questioners might have expected, one "single" commandment, making that the guiding light of all the rest. Instead, he named the *point* of all the commandments; he named the secret goal toward which *every one* of them is oriented.

But what is this point; what is this goal? Basically just this one thing: that we belong to God with all our heart, all our soul, and all the strength of our mind. However, we don't do that naturally. And since we don't do it, our heart is divided. That is the root of our misery.

It is clear when we look at ourselves that we continually put God off with installment payments and give him "something" of ourselves in a piecemeal fashion; but we hardly give ourselves. We allow him a worship service, perhaps, in which we participate. We hear the eternal words and let him have a few scraps of prayer in the bargain. But hardly are we outside before totally different cares and hopes crowd in upon us. This divided life wears us down. We cannot find rest. It would be more fortunate, perhaps, for a person to be *totally* blind and *totally* deaf to eternal things, since he would not even begin to subject himself to this bifurcation. But we are people who jump from the operating table before the operation is over. And those people are the most pathetic of all. He who only half gives himself to God is always cheated. He would have been better off not to have started in the first place.

That is precisely the reason that Jesus alludes to the "whole" heart, that is, a heart redeemed from inner division. *We find happiness only when we will one thing.*

But how is it possible for us to "will one thing" (Kierkegaard)? It is possible only in that *love* that our text refers to: If you love anyone—and only then!—you are totally there for the other person. Then you do not need a sense of duty to wring out some kind act; you do it gladly. One feels downright called upon to do it. It would be ridiculous in a case like that to say, "It's my damned duty and obligation to spend this evening with a person whom I love, while I would much prefer to amuse myself in another way." That would be absurd because I now "want" to do what I "should" do; I am spontaneously impelled to be there with the other person.

That was the problem of the elder brother in Jesus' parable of the prodigal son. He was a faithful man of duty, who had stayed at home like a good fellow and served his father. And now when his straying brother came home destitute, he apparently felt himself somewhat constrained by his "Christian" sense of duty to greet his brother with a forced smile whether he wanted to or not (after all a Christian "ought" not be resentful!). But his heart wasn't in it. Because his heart was divided. With a grunt and a groan he managed to say, "Welcome back." But at the same time it rankled him that the house was filled with the sounds of preparation and the smells of roasting meat for this dubious ne'er-do-well; he secretly calculated what kind of applause *he* ought to get if everyone in the house treated him proportionately.

It was this divided heart that made him so melancholy and miserable. As we said earlier, his heart did not beat in time with the father's heart, which was full of happiness because his lost son had found his way home. Had the elder brother loved the father and been able to rejoice with him, he would have been freed from the division in his heart. He would have become "unambiguous" and thus would have experienced the joy of love.

Happiness, indeed, is nothing else—Kant himself said it— than the conformity of human nature with its goal. It is therefore the harmony of man with himself. Since we are created in the image of *God*, we attain this harmony with ourselves only by being at peace with him, that is, by being able to love him. This was what Augustine meant by his famous words that our hearts are restless until they "rest in God."

When I was a child, we were sometimes naughty and at a loss for something to do, then our bad humor would lead us to think up one foolish thing after another. My mother used to tell us, "Don't be so 'many-willed'!" I have not heard this expression later in life, but it seems to me to express exactly the cause of that self-destructive uneasiness that keeps us running in circles. Our hearts are divided; we are "many-willed," and therefore we are not oriented toward that one thing that is not only needful (Luke 10:42) but is our source of joy.

That is why we do not become happy when we are only *men of duty*—if we force ourselves to pay a few installments on neighborly love, if we fight back a rising feeling of envy or hatred because a Christian supposedly ought not do this and that and *is* in duty bound to do thus and so. That is why we maintain our marriage—out of a sense of duty, of course—even though it has become pretty burdensome. That is why we behave tolerably well toward a colleague even though we really can't stand him. And so we remain constantly pulled this way and that, never becoming wholeheartedly enthusiastic about anything.

Therefore, Jesus here offers us an immense relief. If we could *love God* and were thus in harmony with him, we would be done with those reluctant installment payments of moral duties. For then we would belong to him *totally;* then we would think and feel *with* him. And if you belong totally to anyone, you really can't be phony with him anymore. Then you actually need only go along with your heart, wherever it takes you. All anxious questions cease—whether he demands this or that of me, whether he really resents this or could take offense at that. He who loves stops calculating and abandons his scruples. His heart overflows and he drifts in a refined form of carelessness.

To be able to love God: that would liberate us from the division within our hearts. But then who *is* God that we could love him in this way? Isn't he terribly hidden? Where was he in the lives of those who murdered children during the Nazi time? Where is he in the jungle war in Asia? Where is he in the latest air disaster?

The psalmist asked the same question long ago as he vainly, at first in despair and then wonderfully comforted, sought for the footprints of God in the riddles of human life. "Thy way was through the sea, thy path through the great waters; yet thy footprints were unseen" (Ps. 77:19). We are in fact not able to recognize God's footprints in the sense that we are permitted to "identify" him—his trail is lost in the water. If he is sought here, the trail ends in nihilism. We have him only in the One whom Luther called the "mirror of the fatherly heart," the One who talks to the Pharisees in this text. In him we are met by a love that continued to seek even the misguided executioner who stood under the cross, or the men who cried out from the aroused mob that they wanted "his blood to be upon us and upon our children." Even in the night of Golgotha, when not only the footprints of God melted away, but the very idea of a loving and reigning God was incomprehensible to the human mind, still this love remained visible in the man who hung on the cross and reached out for the Father's hand in that night of meaninglessness. Whoever clings to this sign can remain in love, where he becomes able to discern the peace that enfolds even his divided and quarreling heart.

As people who have experienced God's love and who can look back from his heart to our own restlessness, we can recognize the division in our hearts from many other contemporary symptoms which give us trouble.

One sign of that division is the peculiar situation which is currently designated by the "in" word "uneasiness." This word crops up in conversation about the world political situation, the problems between East and West, the economic climate, and the restlessness of our youth. The analysis of this word "uneasiness" and the causes behind it requires more extensive consideration. At this point I wish to mention just one point of view because it relates to our topic. I mean the question of whether that uneasiness does not also have something to do with what we have called the "divided heart."

On the one hand we hear the message of freedom as a human right, of the free development of personality, of freedom of the press, and many other things. We also see—and one need only think of the many abuses in our news media—how this doctrine of freedom is often carried to excess and misused. On the other hand, we run up against entrenched, immovable institutions, bureaucracies, and power structures, or even the equally rigid opposition of ideologies in East and West. We rub ourselves raw on this unresolvable tension between our freedom and our captivity.

I think of still another form of this division. We have everything we need in the way of consumer goods and more. The stores overflow with Christmas gifts and shoppers; travel agencies offer tours for the "average man" that our grandparents could only dream of. But by having all we need and more, we stand in a peculiar emptiness, without a goal. We have planned super highways well, and soon we will live in a perfect welfare state. But where do these well-planned highways lead? What is the meaning of this well-oiled machine? It was in regard to this question that Albert Einstein once said, "We live in a time of perfect means and confused ends." As long as one fights for the most primitive living conditions and for life itself, as we did during and just after the war, one can be wrapped up in struggling for the means of existence and can forget the question of an ultimate goal. But once one has obtained these essentials and lives fairly comfortably, then the meaning and purpose of this life suddenly become burning issues. And I believe that it can be both the greatness and promise of an historical moment when this question bursts forth with vehemence, even if the forms in which that happens are frequently disagreeable and are stamped by that melancholy "uneasiness" itself.

In any case, that is *again* a division in our hearts, in which we reveal to ourselves the contradiction between what we have achieved and the purposelessness of our lives which confuses us and makes us so dreadfully hopeless.

This uneasiness makes us strike out at everything around us. A person simply *must* lash out and become aggressive if he no longer has confidence in anything. And right in the midst of this restlessness the gospel comes to us, that message of Jesus which counters the division in our hearts with the forces of love and of confidence.

The confidence to which we Christians testify and in which we hope to live and die, does not at all mean that in any situation, no matter how desperate, we should simply keep still and blindly give in to the "higher counsels of God," even if we don't understand a thing. It means, rather, that *by* keeping still and daring to say, "Thy will be done," our confidence reaches out still further. We know that the One in whom we put our trust controls the powers of change sufficiently to change *them*. He is not only with us in the boat; he is also Lord of the powers and elements that are having their way with the little craft. Wind and wave are under his command. Even the thoughts and emotions of the human soul, in fact the peoples of the earth (Ps. 33:10) await his counsel, and "the proud waves" (Job 38:11) must calm down at his behest.

Therefore we may set out confidently into a dim future— simply because the promise has no end. The men of God are always summoned into darkness and uncertainty. Abraham was sent into a land he did not know, and he had nothing with him but the certainty that the promise would accompany him. And we too do not know what the day after tomorrow will bring. We are not to "be anxious about tomorrow"; we are just to take the next step resolutely, certain that the new day cannot impose anything upon us that has not passed the scrutiny of our heavenly Father. Nothing will happen to us or meet us tomorrow or the day after tomorrow that he has not seen and blessed to our use.

Therefore we walk into the dark resolutely and confident as a child, without that fraying division that pulls us back and forth between hope and fear. We walk in that simplicity of heart that keeps our eye on the lilies of the field and the birds of the air.

This confidence, however, also sends us out to *act*, where we fight and struggle for a better world. But we don't live our life without considering our maker. We don't "lose" ourselves in programs or put our confidence in utopias. We know that the world cannot change if our old heart, that deceitful and desperately corrupt thing (Jer. 17:9), is not changed *first*. Nothing but confused thoughts can flow from a heart that has no confidence and that vacillates between hope and fear, haunting anxiety and illusions.

Therefore the summons of Jesus which calls us to love involves more than our personal life and our private relationship to our fellow men. Where hearts and all the powers of human nature are kindled into love, a fire breaks out which bursts all boundaries, invading society, the state, and all that comes in contact with those for whom God is *everything*.

Who dares to count on that? Who dares to trust this promise? God needs persons with whom he can work; men who have been freed to grasp the wonders which he promises us.

10. HOW FREE ARE WE?

For all things are yours . . . and you are Christ's; and Christ is
God's.   *1 Corinthians 3:21, 33*

Whatever your task, work heartily, as serving the Lord and not
men.   *Colossians 3:23*

Anyone who has walked through a prison and talked with
criminals or has witnessed proceedings in a juvenile court cannot
escape asking himself, "Were these people really free when they
committed the crime?" Perhaps they come from an antisocial
environment; perhaps they have never known a person who
could be a trustworthy example for them; perhaps they grew
up without love, left to themselves or to the street, and now
they sit here waiting to be given over to a future without exit.
After one such hearing a juvenile court judge said to me in
despair, "Wouldn't you and I also have ended up where that
young fellow is if we had grown up in a Hell's Kitchen like
that? What right has society to judge in a case like this? Isn't
society itself the defendant when it allows circumstances of that
sort to exist?" Then how free are we—that is the question.

This problem also arises in another form: Are the magazines
and other organs of the press right in calling upon freedom (in
this case "freedom of the press") to protect them when they
pander without inhibition to the sex market or when they
publicize shallow playboys and playgirls as examples to the
young? All this being done for commercial reasons, specifically
to push their circulation figures a little higher by appealing to
instincts that belong in the cellar or toolshed of the human
psyche. How far does freedom, even freedom of the press,
extend?

I have not raised this question in order to undertake the
hopeless task of treating it in one brief chapter. I wish only to

indicate by its use the scope of the considerations that occupy us in dealing with this topic.

Out of the vast complex of questions that arise in this area, I would like to select just a part of one single issue for the present discussion. It is admittedly of special importance, so I will begin by describing it somewhat more precisely.

Both as philosopher and poet, Sartre continually asserted the following thesis in his plays: If a person lives in a tightly knit social system or even in a Christian tradition, he is thereby robbed of his freedom. He is confined in a plethora of "oughts" and rules. From all sides he hears, "Thou shalt this and that; thou ought not do thus and so." People have definite expectations of me, and these pin me down; they "fix" me. Thus, claims Sartre, a person never comes to himself, he never reaches his own identity; he simply goes on following another's will. He can never become an "original"; he constantly runs around as a "copy."

True freedom is to be found only where a person "posits" himself, that is, where he autonomously decides what he will be and where he therefore himself and by his own will decides what he considers his duty to be. In the play *The Flies*, Orestes struggles through everything that would pin him down and fix him, saying pathetically, "I am my freedom." By that he meant, "I am not the object from which others want something. Nor am I the object of an historical combination of guilt and fate. I am the autocratic *subject* of my future; I am master in the house of my ego; I write the novel of my own life and don't let other people dictate it to me. I don't let others paint my portrait; I paint it myself."

Sartre knows very well that this sort of freedom is a hardship. He goes so far as to say that we are "condemned" to freedom. That means that we really prefer *not* to exercise this degree of self-determination. It puts an enormous responsibility on us. It is much easier and more comfortable to be able to follow the schedule of predetermined commandments. Then we need only live up to what is expected of us and do whatever agrees with the traditional value system. Then we need only conform and simply cooperate. That is a tremendous saving of energy in itself. We don't need to beat our brains out so much (others will do that for us) and we don't have to make as many decisions for ourselves.

From our observations of refugees from East Germany, we could occasionally discern what a hardship it can be when anyone from a tightly knit system that prescribes every step for him is suddenly expelled (actually "expelled") into freedom. It seems to him that he has been dumped into a vacuum and he doesn't know what he is to do with himself.

Thus orders and commandments or a fixed, prescribed itinerary are often very much more comfortable and therefore also more desirable, even if such imperatives go against my grain and cause me to moan about the restriction of my freedom.

This insight also enables us to explain the fascination which the so-called legalistic religions have always exercised. They wish to squeeze existence into a very narrow structure. Yet within this structure there is more than coercion and "repression," there is also security. A person need not make his way through the adventure-lands of life by relying on his own compass; he can move through fenced-in spaces and along beaten paths where he will be led by experienced hands.

If Sartre thinks that he has struck at Christianity with these principles, and that he is resisting all the regimentation which the so-called commandments of God expect of us, then he is in error. He seems to have no idea of the extent to which he himself is a secular follower of this Christian faith.

Prescriptions are precisely *not* where the message of Jesus begins. It does not begin, as Kant does, with the imperative "thou shalt." No, first of all, long before anything is demanded of me, I receive the necessary equipment which enables me to satisfy the will of God. At the very beginning something is *given* to me.

When I encounter Jesus Christ, I learn two things in the first act of this new and immensely exciting part of my life: *First*, everything starts when I hear the call, "I have called you by name, you are mine" (Isa. 43:1). I also learn that God is not indifferent to me, that he calls to me, and that it concerns him when I wander lost in the far country. It is as though he lays his hand on my shoulder and tells me, "I am still here for you, don't you see that?"

And then the *second* thing that gives my life a new twist is that I hear him say, "You are near and dear to me. I am not offended by the fact that your reputation is questionable or that you have a skeleton in your closet or spots on your vest. In fact I want to pull you out of the dismal hole in which you crouch so helplessly. I want you to share in the freedom that nearness to me provides, for you are dear to me and close to my heart."

This news actually brings totally new impulses into my life. If I learn that anyone thinks of me with an affection that shares my lot and perhaps even suffers with me, then thankfulness streams back to him from *my* side and I am impelled to do something to please him. Thus an exchange takes place. It is like a lively circuit which is released between electrical poles. It is quite spontaneous and flows "completely of itself" from an inner impulse. There doesn't have to be a commandment that expressly orders it to happen. How grotesque it would be, for example, if a mother would order her child, "Now love me for once!" If the child detects that the mother loves him from her heart, that she spends time and energy on him (and not from some "damned duty and obligation," but because her *heart* urges her to do it), then the child, on his part, will respond with spontaneously answering affection. Thus the circuit of alternating love begins to flow.

Answering and spontaneous love of this kind is naturally something completely different from a mere feeling of "sympathy." It involves the whole man. That means it also leads to *action*. A person who loves wishes to *do* something to please the beloved. But *what* he does under those circumstances need not be elicited by a command or put under a rule. It can be quite irregular, unusual, and contrary to a commandment while still remaining within the circuit of love. A young mother once recounted to me that she had spent much time and expense on new wallpaper for her house. Then, when she had gone out for a moment to shop, little Inge had made an unimaginable mess on the walls with crayons. When she returned, Inge presented

143

her with this product and beamed, "Look what I painted for you, mother!" "For you," she said—and these two words had choked off the anger which was welling up within her. The little girl had, in her own way, painted a declaration of love on the wall, and the mother had recognized it amidst the scribbling, even though the childish scrawl was contrary to rules and orderliness and involved some trouble for the mother. The child had used her freedom (really freedom!) to tell the mother in her own way that she had waited lovingly and eagerly for her to come home. And despite her irritation over the wallpaper, that love was more important to the mother than rigidly channeled obedience and routine good behavior. She said to herself, "If only the child loves me, she shall have the freedom to express that love in her own way." Then the forms in which that love is clothed may be left to her childish judgment, even when they are peculiar.

That is precisely the point made by the scriptural texts which report Jesus' exposition of the commandment about the Sabbath. How could he dare to brush aside cultic prescriptions so regally? Why should he cross out the books of the law, just like that child brushing aside those rules of good manners which said that one ought not scribble on walls? The reason he could ignore the ceremonial Sabbath commandment was that his love for his Father (which included love for his hungry companions) gave him the freedom to put the *spirit* of the Sabbath law above the *letter* of its prescriptions. This spirit, of course, affirms that the Sabbath exists for *man* and not man for the Sabbath. It says that God thus wanted to serve man through a day of rest (Mark 2:23–28).

When anyone returns this love of God, he receives freedom— the freedom to decide on his own responsibility what God intends and then to do it. In this way he is empowered to disregard the casuist's detailed stipulations with a sovereign freedom. God does not want men to go hungry; therefore a person ought not be a hair-splitter and let men continue to hunger just because a commandment that is valid under normal conditions appears to forbid the plucking of grain on the Sabbath. Where love is, there is also the freedom to choose and to make one's own decision. Therefore Augustine once said, "Love, and then do what you please."

The consequences, however, extend much farther. I just said that the gospel, indeed the whole Bible, is full of hints, reports, and assurances that God cares about us and that our lostness and our return home move him deeply, even to the degree that he took the pain of Golgotha upon himself for that reason. Doesn't that have to motivate us to open *our* hearts to him?

But if we thus love God in return, then something enters the picture that also has its parallels on the human level. If I am bound to a person in love, then *his* worries are *my* worries and his joy makes *me* happy too. Then it is unavoidable that what concerns him and commands his ultimate loyalty would also become a concern of mine and would in no instance leave me indifferent. Then what concerns God? He is involved—we have said it once before—with me and my fellow men; he keeps watch over his lost, unhappy, and guilty children. How then could it be otherwise? This love of his passes on to me, so that it literally puts me on, and thus a flow is established from the origin of all love and forgiveness, from that which God does for me and for us all, through me to my neighbor (see Matt. 18:21–35).

Therefore it is only natural that Jesus Christ speaks of love of God and the neighbor in the same breath, binding the two together. As soon as I love God my neighbor becomes my deepest concern—simply because he concerns God. That was the tragedy of the elder brother in Jesus' parable of the prodigal son (the image of this figure forces itself upon us again and again). He could not understand why his father was moved by the return of the younger son from his straying in the far country and why he arranged a rousing banquet for him. He was left cold by the thing that warmed his father's heart. Thus his indifference to his brother was at the same time a sign that he didn't love his father either; the circuit between his heart and his father's was broken.

When, however, this circuit, this flow to the neighbor begins, then the scope of freedom is once again widened. Then I, on my own responsibility and at my own risk, must figure out what serves my neighbor and what I therefore owe him.

At the Catholic Pastoral Congress in Holland (which aroused such a great sensation in the European press) Eduard Schillebeekx, the theologian, rightly said that, according to Christian ethics, the moral mastery of existence is not prescribed by eternally valid rules, ordinances, and commandments. Love is the sole standard—understood as that very specific sort of love that appears in Jesus Christ. Jesus, as well as Paul and even the Old Testament, had simply translated this basic commandment into the norms and value systems of *their* time. Therefore, we ought not set up their legal systems as absolutes, presuming in the name of faith to take them upon ourselves. It is our task, upon our own freely activated responsibility, to bring this commandment of love for God and the neighbor to bear upon the structures of *our* life and our society.

Doesn't this point of view somehow liberalize and soften the commandment? Doesn't this approach put everything up in the air? Don't we lose our bearings completely, without any fixed standards?

That opinion would be quite wrong. On the contrary, this approach involves a much more radical obedience to the call of God than that of merely following mechanically certain rules and commandments. If I just follow the rules, my heart can remain aloof; I need only "search" for him outwardly, so I can dispense with any inner involvement. And that is exactly what the Lord does *not* want; he wants *all* of me.

At crucial points in the Bible, therefore, Jesus refuses to give us very definite and detailed rules of behavior. It would be far too simple to follow them; all you would have to do would be to pull your belt a little tighter; otherwise, though, you could remain completely uninvolved. You could be "miles away" inwardly. Instead of these rules, Jesus unlocks the much more strenuous world of freedom to us and lets us decide for ourselves which way of obedience we think is demanded of us.

I will illustrate that with a single example, although many are available.

Once the Pharisees wanted to lay a trap for him and so they

asked him the question about whether taxes should be paid to Caesar. That was a highly explosive political question to which one could only give a wrong answer, one that might even endanger one's life. No matter what one said, it was bound to be taken amiss. However, Jesus answered, "Render therefore to Caesar the things that are Caesar's, and to God the things that are God's" (Matt. 22:21).

Thus there is no rule of behavior according to which the competing jurisdictions of God and Caesar, church and state, can be marked off precisely and cleanly delimited. Such a rule would suit people, because it would be so simple to be bound by a regulation and thus have the burden of a personal decision lifted from one's shoulders. But Jesus leaves the question of the competing jurisdictions wide open. He thereby opens a zone of freedom which compels us (yes, freedom compels us!) to decide on our own responsibility out of our love for God how we will resolve, in each instance, the conflict between what God demands of us and what Caesar, state, and society want from us.

By expecting that of us, Jesus releases in us what Kierkegaard called the "infinite passion of inwardness." For now we can't get by with upright forms of outward correctness and faithfulness to rules. Now God wants us totally. He wants our understanding; he wants the exertion of our thought-processes; he wants our struggle for the right path; he wants—to use the words of the Bible itself (Deut. 6:5)—all our heart, all our soul, and all our strength, even our mental strength, the "power of reflection" as we like to call it today. Therefore God does not desire robots of obedience, who only react mechanically; he lays claim to our mental potential, the total effort of our minds.

The freedom that love gives to us is actually strenuous and demanding, because it is always harder to give myself *completely* than only to give myself *halfway*. And God wants us completely. There is no doubt that this freedom of love opens up many possible varieties of action, and that thus on an individual basis the most sharply differing decisions could grow out of it. Therefore the activity of a Christian is not rigid and "nailed down." It is flexible; there are no tracks running from A to Z that lay out the way we must go. In many matters we will decide differently from our parents and grandparents, even though we operate within the framework of the same commandment to love. That commandment binds all of us, from the patriarchs and prophets right up until today and on into the future.

But isn't that (to repeat the question which was raised earlier) still a liberal softening of the obedience demanded of the Christian? Doesn't that lead to dangerous laxity?

At this point in our consideration the quotation of Paul which I placed at the beginning of this chapter can make a contribution: "All things are yours . . . and you are Christ's." "All is yours"—that means that you have unlimited rights of control and unlimited scope for your freedom. There are no "taboos" for you. Yet you can only claim these privileges of freedom when you are and remain bound to him who gives them to you. Therefore, all things are yours *only* because you are Christ's. Without him your freedom would in fact become license and would degenerate into arbitrariness. With him, however, and bound to him, our love presses toward quite specific forms of actualization, even though our freedom still has the task of finding those forms.

That is easy to see. Perhaps I can't stand a co-worker of mine. He may even be outspokenly unsympathetic to me. Then my natural tendency would be to ignore him, to avoid him, or to snap at him. If I am Christ's, however, then I know that Jesus Christ is interested in this person who is so alien to me. I know that he turns to him in love and even offers himself for him. If I take over this love of his into my own life, this co-worker can no longer leave me unconcerned. I am forced to ask myself if, in the eyes of Jesus, I am really any more sympathetic a companion than my co-worker is. Jesus Christ, however, has found his way to me. Doesn't that constrain me, in turn, to move in my brother's direction?

Perhaps, to cite another instance of this sort—politics is anathema to me. I am allergic to politics because the influence-peddling, mistrust, and power hunger in this field offend me. I am thoroughly convinced that the game of politics is really a dirty game. But then suddenly I discover that political activity and structures have a profound effect on my neighbor's life. The educational system has a powerful influence on the future of young people; the social order literally has the power of life and death over pensioners, invalids, and dependents; the execution of punishment decides what will become of human brothers and sisters who turned to crime (will they find their way back into society, or will they remain outcasts?). And I cannot even remain indifferent to the fact that the long- or short-range effects of politics force men in Africa or Asia into hunger, misery, and death.

If the love of Jesus permeates me, and if he has opened my eyes to my neighbor, then that political sector (which, as was said, may leave me cold) is laid on my conscience. I then realize that I serve none less than the Lord himself when I cease to stand aloof and become involved as far as my influence and possessions will permit. But here again it is like the story of the tax money: No specific political route is prescribed for me; the Bible does not put a prefabricated rule of conduct in my hands or direct me to a certain political party. It is rather love that once more opens the realm of freedom to me. In that realm, which claims my whole heart and all the powers of my mind, I am to search out what decisions God demands of me here and now. God does not merely want my will, which simply nods and does what it is told. He also wants my reason; he wants my emotions and everything I have and am, so that I place it all at his disposal. That is how free we are—and how bound.

In closing, I would like to clarify what I mean by that through an illustration.

If I am a follower of Jesus, on the one hand, I cannot extract from the Gospel legalistic rules of conduct and detailed standards which lead me along step by step. On the other hand, I am not left without *any* instruction, simply given over to my subjective and arbitrary will, so that I end up with—as the popular term puts it—a purely "situational ethic." Rather (and now I am using the clarifying illustration) the Bible does not press a road map into my hands with the way I am to go marked out beforehand. The crossroads are not noted in advance with instructions about whether I am to go to the right or the left. I cannot read from the supposed road map of the Bible, therefore, what I should decide about questions like birth control, abortion, homosexuality, the pill, the death penalty, or—in a totally different area—participatory management of industry. If I could mechanically read off the solutions to all these questions, I would only have once again become obedient to an alien will. I myself would not be touched by the demand and the call for involvement.

And yet I am not completely left dangling even when I don't have those prefabricated decisions to fall back upon. I am not completely bereft of all directions which I so urgently need in order to get my bearings. But what marching order do I have left?

Suppose that, instead of a map, I am given a *compass* and then sent out. The compass needle points to the commandment about loving God and the neighbor. This, therefore, is the direction I have to go. At every crossroad I am faced with the question of which way will enable me to hold to the indicated direction. *But I myself must find the way.* That is my freedom; it is also the *burden* of that freedom. For I can't just steadfastly and stubbornly march straight ahead as I follow the compass's direction. The way has rivers, mountains, and other rough terrain which I must get around. Stripped of imagery, that means that the direction I go is influenced by the situations in which I find myself at any given time; I may live in a dictatorship or a democracy; I may be sick and must take care of myself; perhaps I want to join the Peace Corps and work in underdeveloped countries, but I have a family that needs me too. One can name a long list of genuine considerations, impediments, and conflicts of duty which make it flatly impossible to charge on straight ahead without looking to the left or to the right. And these hindrances are exactly parallel to the streams and rivers that lie in my way when I follow the compass needle. I must go around them. Thus sometimes I have to pause and consider. The compass direction leaves me free to pause in that way and even to be inventive and independent in the attempt to conquer the rough terrain in my life and to get around it. But this freedom is also a burden, and that is as it should be. For I ought not wander about the countryside aimlessly in the name of freedom; through all my zig-zagging and roundabout travel I must keep my eye on the compass needle. The whole countryside is mine; that is my freedom; but I am Christ's, and his love "controls" and leads me (2 Cor. 5:14).

That is the latitude of venture and freedom I am given: *I myself must find the ways to the goals which God has set for me in the commandment to love.*

Obviously I cannot find these ways without him who also sets the goals. They are *his* goals. And he is not only the Lord of the *goals*, but also Lord of the *ways*. Therefore I seek these often quite indiscernible ways in the fog and in the dark valley, while I ask the Lord of the goals and ways for proper guidance, entrusting my helplessness to him:

> I am weak, but thou art mighty,
> Hold me with thy powerful hand.[1]

He is my rod and staff; he throws bridges across the chasms I fear and consider impassable.

> Heavenly Leader still direct us,
> Still support, console, protect us.[2]

Thus I walk like a child into the darkness, holding a hand that shepherds me. With this request for proper guidance I venture on my way, trusting the promise that I will not be brought low.

To be permitted so to choose under the commandment of love, to be given such a limitless gift of personal responsibility—that is my freedom; that is the *noblesse oblige* of the children of God. That is a nobility that lays claim to their whole heart and also to all the faculties of their mind. That is how free we are—and how bound.

1. William Williams, "Guide me, O thou great Jehovah."
2. Nicolaus Ludwig von Zinzendorf, "Jesus still lead on."

11. HOW CAN GOD AND POLITICS MIX?

The scribes and the chief priests . . . watched him, and sent spies, who pretended to be sincere, that they might take hold of what he said, so as to deliver him up to the authority and jurisdiction of the governor.

They asked him, "Teacher, we know that you speak and teach rightly, and show no partiality, but truly teach the way of God. Is it lawful for us to give tribute to Caesar, or not?"

But he perceived their craftiness, and said to them, "Show me a coin. Whose likeness and inscription has it?"

They said, "Caesar's."

He said to them, "Then render to Caesar the things that are Caesar's, and to God the things that are God's."

And they were not able in the presence of the people to catch him by what he said; but marveling at his answer they were silent.

Luke 20:19–26

The topic of religion and politics is almost as old as mankind itself. I remember a story out of the dim past: In a famous tragedy of Sophocles, Antigone buried the body of her dead brother. She did it even though the king had strictly forbidden the burial and had threatened violators with dire punishment. She defended her disobedience by citing the "eternal unwritten law" which demanded respect for the dead. In that way she openly asserted that this religious commandment to bury the dead was more important and held a higher rank than the decrees of earthly authorities.

The same thing has happened again and again: When Luther stood up to face the emperor at Worms and said, "Here I stand, I cannot do otherwise," and when the aged Bishop Wurm told Himmler, who was then leader of Hitler's elite troops, that mass murder was contrary to the command of God and that Himmler would one day have to answer for it before the bar of the last judgment, these cases were simply variations

152

on an age-old theme encompassing the poles of God and Caesar, eternal and earthly authority, religion and politics, love and power.

Thick books could be written on that topic. That is because it involves a problem for which there is no pat solution. The conflict between the two powers certainly does not arise out of malice or megalomania. Sometimes, even with the best will in the world, it is not at all easy to say where the line runs between what God commands and what we owe to earthly authorities—to the state, to our boss, to our professional duties, and to our business. During the Nazi persecution of the Jews, for example, should Pope Pius XII take politics and tactics into consideration, should he keep silent for opportunistic reasons in order to prevent worse things from happening? Or should he cry out in the name of God, without a glance at the consequences, to the world about the injustice, even when the whole structure of his church would be shaken because of his act? What does he owe to *politics* and what does he owe to *God*? What does he owe to the interests of his institution—for "interests" is what politics is all about—and what does he owe to merciful love with its stress on sacrifice? (That is the problem that Hochhuth dealt with, although not with complete success, in his play *The Deputy*.)

But we don't need to think only about politics at the national level; our own little lives offer examples enough. Am I obliged, for example, to render military service when the state demands it, if I personally am a pacifist and live by the word of Jesus? "All who take the sword will perish by the sword" (Matt. 26:52). That involves not merely draft-dodgers, but often very earnest people who worry about this question. If we think about the inhabitants of ideological dictatorships, this problem reaches an almost deadly acuteness: Ought we to be loyal to a state whose schools warp the souls of our children, destroy their faith, and drill them in hypocrisy?

What do I owe to God and what to the state—to *this* state? That is the question.

Our text today takes a stand on this problem. But it doesn't hand us a slick solution on a silver tray. It gives us no patent medicine which will help to lift all further thought on the matter from our minds. On the contrary, it is worth giving thought to what the text leaves open and *why* it does so.

The first thing to observe in our text is that the conversation recorded here does not take place on neutral academic ground, where a problem can be talked out with calmness and objectivity. This text involves an almost elemental threat, a provocation, it involves being and nonbeing. By means of this problem of "religion and politics" someone is to be done away with and liquidated. There is no theorizing here; it is a matter of life and death. And to that extent this story, right down to its style, is a very precise model by which one can study the course of such disputations.

For once the question of religion and politics really becomes acute, then it usually does not occur in the calm of an auditorium, but in encounter of a Dibelius and Ulbricht, a Niemöller and Hitler, Nathan and David, John and Herod, or even Thomas à Becket and Henry II (in Anouilh's drama) [or: in Eliot's *Murder in the Cathedral*]. And wherever that happens the one of the two who represent God usually has more at stake than the solution of a problem—a "brainteaser." He has put his neck on the block; it involves faithfulness and denial, which means his temporal and eternal fate. It can be truly said that this question thrives only at high temperatures and when the parties pick a hot spot for their fight.

Thus the situation is ominous from the first moment, even though Jesus' opponents start out by trying to make an innocent impression, hoping thereby to lull him into false assurance. The people, every one of them paid spies or tools, act as if they were interested in a real discussion. They want to deal with the problem of "religion and politics." But they know that discussion of a problem like that can go on endlessly, and a clever debater is hard to pin down in a theoretical dispute—as long as he doesn't want to be pinned down. Then everything is left up in the air and hypothesized to death. In order to avoid a draw of that sort, the agents of the Pharisees make known that they want to discuss a question of *conscience* (and then no merely theoretical problem). They want to talk about the ethical aspects of politics. And admittedly one must answer a question of conscience without "ifs, ands, or buts" and without loopholes and gamesmanship. One must say "yea, yea" or "nay, nay." A question of conscience does not permit one to operate on the basis of "tactics." Therefore someone can be pinned down in this area with particular effectiveness.

The people start right off with this goal in mind by beginning with a little flattery, "Master, we know that you are matchless in word and teaching. You look neither to the right nor the left; you are no opportunist. Of course you can afford the harshness of this straight-and-narrow because you have no anxiety and because you are only concerned about God. Therefore we can count on your giving us an answer to the question of conscience that we pose to you, and we know that it will not be an involved answer, hedged on all sides, but that it will be without horns and teeth; direct, massive, and *straight*, just as your conscience dictates."

Thus they challenge the Lord precisely at the crucial point of his calling as Savior—at that point where his conscience indeed bids him to scorn the fear of men and let himself be governed only by love of his Father and of his human brothers. If he gives in here—if he does play the "tactics" and looks for "academic" loopholes, then he has already lost the game. Then he has betrayed his calling.

If, on the contrary, he takes his calling seriously and comes out with a clear decision, spurning any tactical smokescreens, then he is lost for sure. For the question as posed is subtly formulated to make the person questioned hang himself.

This question, of course, was, "Ought we pay taxes to the Roman emperor or not?" There seems to be no way out of this noose.

If he says, "Pay the tax," he has betrayed his people. His countrymen groaned under the Roman occupation forces, while they worked passionately for national self-determination. And Jesus' answer would thus plead the cause of the occupation forces and their tyranny. In that way he would have brought ostracism as an enemy of the people upon his own head.

If, however, he would answer, "You don't need to pay the

emperor any tax *at all*," then he would hand himself over to the *Romans*, since he had committed an act of sabotage against the actual legal rulers. "Well, Jesus of Nazareth," the opponents think (without coming out and saying it, of course), "root hog or die. You won't get out of this trap alive." For as we said before, they addressed his conscience and thereby blocked him from escaping this either-or by some debater's tactic.

Now it is impressive to see how Jesus does not mar the "advice-to-stricken-consciences" character of his answer in the slightest, but nevertheless he silences the hypocrites who tried to trap him. He orders them to hand him a denarius, a small silver coin, and asks them, "Whose picture and whose name are stamped there?" When they have to answer, "Caesar's picture and name," he has compromised them in an ironical way. They have to admit that they themselves receive the emperor's money and use it—in fact this very moment they have pulled it out of their purses. Then they recognize de facto certain sovereign powers of the emperor, for example, finance and taxation. Despite all their religious and political aloofness from Rome, therefore, they still in fact respect a certain modicum of governmental functions relating to the ordering of society, for example, traffic, administration, civil laws, and so forth.

In exactly the same way, citizens of an ideological system of government—even when they consider the atheistic state to be wrong, or no state at all—nevertheless recognize its speed limits, its foreign exchange rates, and its tax laws. For everyone knows that even an unrighteous state must bear responsibility for a minimum of order and sustenance of life. To that extent it still is better than complete chaos.

Really, these people were badly compromised by having the tribute money in their own pockets, because they were thereby convicted of *already* having made a decision, and therefore they were in no position to pose the question of "religion and politics" from an uncommitted, neutral "vacuum." And so with one blow and an amazing grip they were pinned to the mat. Without a moment's hesitation Jesus follows up his advantage and presses his opponents further. "Therefore," he says, "be logical and give to Caesar what belongs to him, and give God what belongs to him." That means: "*If* you thus must pay tribute to earthly powers (and in fact do pay it, as your money indicates!), then don't forget to give your tribute to *God* as well, not only by praying to him and visiting the temple, but by telling the state, in the name of God, what its obligation is and where its limits lie. On the one hand, respect the state for the order that it brings, but at the same time, let your confession protect it from unknowingly becoming a 'total state' and permitting the emperor to become a god-emperor. Woe unto you, if you, the servant of God, do *not* tell the state what it is and what it owes to God. Woe unto you, if at the last judgment a dictator—a Hitler or an Ulbricht—confronts you with the accusation, 'Granted, I overstepped my bounds; I erected an ideological tyranny, I have overthrown the altars of God and thrown God's witnesses into prison. But it was possible to do what I did only because the church that I persecuted was a society of dumb oxen, of opportunists and quislings that I simply couldn't take seriously. They equated throne and altar, and thus by submissiveness and cringing they tried to take your sheep out of harm's way.' "

Jesus thus lets them know: "If you really give God what belongs to him, then that will not occur in your hymn-singing and your church services. It must also extend to the emperor. You must bear your message into public life; you must be the salt of the earth. You must perform a service of love to the representatives of the state, even tyrants, by warning them in the name of God and communicating to them the truth that has been entrusted to you."

These words that thunder against the spies who thought themselves to be the better trap-setters are, admittedly, somewhat undecided and have a peculiar flexibility. "Give to Caesar what belongs to him, and to God what belongs to him." That leaves the details wide open, doesn't it? Jesus refuses to set up two neatly divided lists of duties relating to God and Caesar ("thou shalt this and not this" or "you may this and not that"). The question about *what* specifically belongs to Caesar and what to God remains open. I must decide that for myself anew in each new situation.

Perhaps it is a little hard on us, perhaps we feel overburdened when Jesus doesn't make this decision once and for all, authoritatively setting up limits; instead, he expects us to make the decision *ourselves*. It sounds somewhat strange, I know, but I must say it nevertheless: the famous "average man" longs for nothing as much as clear, exact, and binding instructions that will, as far as possible, relieve him of making his own decisions. Part of the fascination of Catholic moral theology is that one is given clear and quite detailed rules which demand obedience instead of decision. Thus, for example, one is relieved of the hardship of deciding on Sunday morning whether or not one will go to church, one simply *must* go. Granted, even an obedience of this sort can be trying (for example, when one must get out of bed in the morning!); but it is still not *as* trying as when one must also make the decision whether or not to be obedient or even what *form* that obedience should take. Clear orders and detailed directions for accomplishing them cut the hardship in half. If, on the other hand, one is put on his own, without orders, and has to work out the way of obedience first, then that means doing double duty.

And that is precisely what Jesus Christ actually expects of us when he does not clearly delimit the jurisdiction of God and Caesar; he challenges us to find that out for ourselves again and again as each new occasion arises.

Why does Jesus do that? Why does he make it so hard for us— and particularly hard for those who deal daily with an atheistic ideological state and who simply don't know what a clear decision looks like? Should they, for example, join an agricultural production collective or not? Should they make an issue of the youth dedication of their children or not? How indescribably soothing it could be to have exact recipes and instructions, even if there still would be danger enough in acting accordingly. But at least one would have things put to him straight and would know where he stood.

So we ask again, why does Jesus leave the question of jurisdiction up in the air? Why is he content with the skeletal statement, "Give Caesar what belongs to him, and to God what belongs to him"? This question touches the mystery of our ethical decisions in general, and we must ponder a moment on the basic principles involved.

Anyone facing a serious moral decision (for example, whether he should tell a lie, or whether he should reveal to a very sick friend that he must die, or whether he should keep silent) knows that it is not that easy to be clear on what to do. Sometimes one is inclined to say: In this case things are so complicated and so many other factors are involved, that I could study every ethical textbook from cover to cover without ever finding this precise situation. As long as matters are merely viewed "generally" or "in principle," everything appears relatively simple and clear. That can be shown in reference to our text.

"In principle" the Jewish people obviously were entitled to national independence; they should not have been enslaved by the heathen state and its emperor. But unfortunately things are never so nice and clear in practice as they seem in theory. What happens, for example, if the Jewish people *is* already in fact dependent upon the Roman emperor—when one is no longer asked if he *wants* the subjugation but already *is* subject? Then one is faced with much more complicated decisions; then one must decide day by day whether he can cooperate with this or that; he must decide what his duty and obligation appear to be here and now, under the given circumstances.

One more example: In principle it is easy to be against Communism; it is no trick at all for us here in the West. But what happens when one *lives*, as seventeen million Germans do, under the influence of Communism without being able to leave? How does the so-called decision against Communism look from *that* perspective? Under those circumstances it would be ridiculously banal and also mortally dangerous simply to be "against" in principle. Instead I must—and this is the part that wears one down—make new decisions on specific issues every day. I must be continually weighing and judging if I can still cooperate with *this* measure, but have to get out of *that* organization. Again and again, often "playing it by ear," I have to conclude whether I can sit out a propaganda speech or

159

whether I must ostentatiously leave the hall; whether I must protest against an atheistic school celebration or whether I should keep still for the sake of my children's future. *Those* are the agonizing decisions that are involved in such circumstances; and they occur in a milder form in the lives of us all.

The mental struggles that we observe in the more serious of our critical young people show us that we face similar decisions. "Ought we, for example," they ask themselves, "work for a mere 'reform' of our social system? Wouldn't that simply perpetuate it and treat only a few symptoms? Wouldn't it be better to raise revolutionary questions about the system as a whole, choosing correspondingly radical methods for the battle?" Here again conflicts arise which are not to be resolved by unequivocal commandments or instructions.

Furthermore, it is easy to be against nuclear bombs in principle; who isn't? But what if the enemy *has* them? Must I, as a Christian, be prepared to renounce these weapons, or must I, precisely *because* I am against the bomb, use it as a deterrent and a preventative against a nuclear war. I only ask, but even the question is frightening! How gladly we would thumb through the Bible to find a crisp and clear, prefabricated answer.

So it is with all questions. While they are on the drawing-board they seem to be perfectly clear, but they suddenly take on a different cast when they are posed in the practical world of reality. And it is no different with the commandments of God, even though they seem in themselves to be so clear.

The meaning of "Thou shalt not commit adultery" is more than clear, of course. But just a minute, what if I *have* committed adultery and have intruded into the life of another woman? Haven't I thereby assumed obligations to *her*; haven't I bound her life to mine so that she would be mortally wounded if I now simply left her for the sake of that commandment? I mention that, not to maintain that a person must behave a certain way in that case, but only to indicate what a burden of responsible decision-making is laid upon us in a practical situation. I also want to point out that the commandment is not simply a train schedule by which one can be hustled from point to point at little cost or effort. Our marriage service speaks of practicing "faithfulness and sincerity" forever. That is not only hard to *do*. It is still harder to figure out in a concrete case what *is* faithful and sincere.

This text sheds light, therefore, far beyond the topic of religion and politics. It shows us that everywhere in our life—in our marriage, in visiting the sick, as a teacher in school, as an employer with his employees, as a businessman with his tax declaration—we have to pose the question anew each day: How and in what way do we practice our obedience to God's commandments today? This question cannot be answered by reference to Schedule C. There is no dictionary in which I could look up what I have to do here and now to please God. Rather I myself must bear the burden of a responsible decision. Often enough it becomes clear to me that in this or that case no slick solution is possible—that perhaps I must choose the lesser of two evils, and that I can only live in the assurance of forgiveness for everything that remains piecemeal and sinful.

Once again: Why does God make it so difficult for us? That now becomes the decisive question. But we know, of course, that the burden God lays upon us is always creative, pointing to a goal that it pursues—a goal that only the burdened achieve. The grasshoppers jump around free and unencumbered, but they never make it.

If God does not give us a list of laws and detailed directions for carrying them out, if he does not lead us around by the nose in the most minor matters, he desires to make us into mature sons, confident that we love him and that in this love we will discover the right thing to do. Here we once more come upon (from a different angle) the profound statement of Augustine, "Love, and then do what you like."

If you love someone very much, you want to see everything through his eyes. And what I do out of this love—no matter what and how it is—will be accepted by the other as a sign of this love of mine. Granted, it may sometimes be questionable from an objective point of view, but that hardly matters. Earlier I recounted the story of the little girl who wanted to surprise her mother by painting her brand-new wallpaper, which had cost hard-earned money, with a rather scribbly picture. Certainly that is objectively wrong. Yet the mother sees, as we tried to point out, the sign of love rather than the marred wallpaper. Our heavenly Father does exactly the same thing with our bungles and questionable decisions if only we do them out of love for him and out of a desire to do what is right.

Having said that, we cannot ignore the fact that the parable of the little girl is lame in one respect—it leaves us in the lurch. The mature, rationally responsible person who loves God cannot simply talk his way out of his foolishness (his wallpaper scribbling) on the basis of naïveté. He who loves and is therefore involved with his whole heart does not remain naïve by any means because he knows that every dimension of his being is required. He who knows that God loves him and therefore desires to love God in return considers himself expressly challenged to think through the *how* and the *form* of his love. God does not bombard me with instructions for carrying out his commandments in every possible case, so that I could follow them blindly and mindlessly, because he prefers to require only one thing of me—that I love him. Precisely for this reason he demands "deliberation" from me; he demands the commitment of my mind and not merely the obedience of my mechanically guided hands.

That is the reason that he requires the decision of our obedience from us afresh every day—so that every day we ask for him afresh and consider how we can seriously live out our life and our love before him. Every morning when I get up I must be prepared to resolve: Today I would like for God to win a victory in my life. Today I do not want to live and act in the easiest and most opportune way for me; I would rather be able to say this evening: "By doing this or that I may have burned my fingers or done myself a disservice. I would have been easier on myself if I had shaved a little off my tax declaration, or if I had not been so careful about the truth in an unpleasant matter, or if I had kept quiet when they told dirty jokes at the service club meeting. It would have been easier for me to take advantage of the opportunity for an amorous adventure, for me to have told myself, 'What difference does it make to me what becomes of her? I'll never see her again.' But in that critical moment I wanted to give God a chance in my life. By deciding for the more difficult way, I have rendered him a little 'thank you' for the sacrifice he has made for me. For a moment I returned his love in deed and in truth. And I am certain that he will forgive me if that was still only halfway, and fragmentary, and left a lot to be desired."

Thus God does not put the burden of decision on us to make things hard for us; he does it to help us be much more *explicit* in our search for him and in our efforts to make him the center of our lives. For it is no longer enough to have a couple of free-floating pious thoughts—pious flesh doesn't count for much; now I am to take God into my everyday life. Now he is to be in every word, every handshake, and every encounter that I have with my neighbor or even with a task. Now I must be watchful and on my toes.

Those who travel as legalists according to a predetermined train schedule can sleep in their berths. They don't need to trouble themselves about how they shall reach their goal. The route is nailed down to the last detail; the authorities of the church or the party or the group have seen to that. That is precisely what changes when the disciple of Jesus is called to his mature childhood. Then God gives me the goal of my journey (that I should love him more and more). I, however, must still sit at the throttle, turn on the headlights, and peer through the windshield so that I manage to stay on the right track at the junctions.

Therefore God has my own good in view when he does not lift the burden of decision from me. It is for my benefit that he does not simply tell me what I am to give to Caesar and what to God, but rather contents himself with the command that I should give each his due. He uses that method to keep me awake and on my toes. He wants to be the star to which I look and by which I set my course. Once I love him, I will be able to sort out the respective jurisdictions. I will be very much awake.

We can also see God's same intention for us and our lives in the way Jesus dealt with people. Then too people occasionally groaned and wanted to know, either directly or obliquely: "Why does he make it so difficult for us? If God himself really intends to come to us in this remarkable Nazarene, why did he pick precisely this failure, this provincial figure on the margin of history, this somewhat obscure wandering preacher? Haven't there been much more brilliant figures, Plato and Socrates, for example, to choose from? And why does this Nazarene steadfastly refuse to perform miracles? Why does he draw back from a public demonstration of his claims, why doesn't he accept the kingdoms and nations of the world in the hour of temptation? If only he had done that! Then he would have cut a somewhat more majestic figure, then he would have had a more believable influence, and then he would have made it easier for us to believe that all power was given to him and that we ought to bet our whole life on this one card."

Why, then—that is the real question—does Christ go about incognito? Why does he try so hard (as Bert Brecht might say) for the alienation effect? Why doesn't he want to be recognized, why does he conceal himself in the form of a weakling, a desperate, doomed man?

Kierkegaard has given us a profound answer to that very basic question: He was disguised in misery and lowliness so that only those could find him who searched with infinite passion. If Jesus had actually jumped from the pinnacle of the temple and had performed similar direct demonstrations, then the people would have gone away satisfied. For we aren't excited by anything that is absolutely certain. Nobody flies into a passion when he hears that two times two equals four. That is so obvious that not one single nerve of mine needs to twitch. But when I face the question of whether this *one* figure holds the key to my destiny, of whether literally everything in my life would look different in case it was true that he took away my guilt, conquered my death, and could give me peace—when I face *that* question—then I will become involved in a totally different way in order to penetrate his mystery. And the more enigmatic and unrecognizable he is to me, the more it excites

164

and intrigues me. That is why Jesus wishes to remain incognito, why he guards his messianic secret and why he forbids those who once learn his secret to tell others. Jesus Christ does not want our first decision to be, "I will follow you"; he wants the prior decision to be our learning to say, "You are the Christ, the Son of the living God." Therefore he leaves the question of whether he *is* the Christ open. Therefore he asks so many enigmatic questions and wraps himself in a cloud of mystery. Wherever God disguises himself, he does so with the goal of releasing passionate questioning in us, he wants our highest truth and our decision. Therefore he clears up nothing beforehand, nor does he say, "Behold, here I am." He puts the compass of his Word in our hand and sets us on the path at midnight in order that we may find him and fulfill our tasks.

How unspeakably hidden and enigmatic God sometimes is when he sends us a sorrow that we cannot understand. It forces the doubting question from our lips, "How could God let that happen?" And out of all that we have to endure in such times, one thing we know: He who does not give up but keeps at it has learned in precisely such dark times to seek God with every fiber of his being. He has ultimately found God, has discovered his hand waving to him and graciously grasping him, and has then burst out, "Nevertheless I am continually with thee" (Ps. 73:23). "When you seek me with all your heart, I will be found by you, says the Lord" (Jer. 29:13–14). How else *could* I put my whole heart into my seeking except by knowing that he dwells in darkness and is not lying about on the street, and that his demands are not set down in black and white in the dictionary; *yet he is my future.*

If he is *not* my future, then there is nothing but meaninglessness and a bottomless void. But if he *is* my future, then there is a hand that holds me; there is a heart that thinks of my good; there is a companion who will not depart from me when I one day must depart. It is not a matter of chance or a matter of luck that I settle on one of these two possibilities. In reality I have the promise, "When you seek me with all your heart, I will be found by you." *God wants your whole heart, that is all.* He always wants the whole. Therefore at this point the decisions cannot be partial. He who places only a portion of his heart at God's disposal, so that he can take his religion along too, better leave matters alone. This is a matter of all or nothing. This demands that a person puts himself in the balance. No one gets by without that.

PART THREE:

How to Hope Again

12. FOR WHAT ARE WE WAITING?

And [John's] father Zacharias was filled with the Holy Ghost,
and prophesied, saying,
Blessed be the Lord God of Israel;
For he hath visited and redeemed his people,
And hath raised up an horn of salvation for us
In the house of his servant David;
As he spake by the mouth of his holy prophets, which have been
  since the world began:
  That we should be saved from our enemies, and from the hand
    of all that hate us;
  To perform the mercy promised to our fathers,
  And to remember his holy covenant;
  The oath which he sware to our father Abraham,
  That he would grant unto us, that we, being delivered out of
    the hand of our enemies,
  Might serve him without fear,
  In holiness and righteousness before him, all the days of our life.
  And thou, child, shalt be called the prophet of the Highest:
  For thou shalt go before the face of the Lord to prepare his ways;
  To give knowledge of salvation unto his people
  By the remission of their sins,
  Through the tender mercy of our God;
  Whereby the dayspring from on high hath visited us,
  To give light to them that sit in darkness and in the shadow of
    death,
  To guide our feet into the way of peace.

Luke 1:67-79

This Advent story recounts how decades of ardent longing were
finally fulfilled for Zacharias. He had wished for a son. Now
the improbable happens, and the aged father leans over the
cradle in joy.

So far it all could be a touching and very human story. It
could come from the local section of a newspaper. People who
read it would be prompted to rejoice with the father and express
their good wishes in variations on the theme, "It was worth
waiting for."

Yet the fabric of this story is shot through with enigmatic and confusing threads. I would like to call attention to one of these threads at the very outset.

The child who has just arrived caused an uproar even before his birth and announced himself in a strange way: a messenger of God had proclaimed him in a way that could only be described as mysterious and eerie. He pointed to a life's plan which had been laid out for this child by a higher hand, and to a decision which set him on the path to distant, and as yet unrecognizable, goals. And if the biological origin of this life from parents of such an advanced age was not improbable enough, the prescribed program for this child's future was even more unusual. For according to that plan this child would be elevated to the "Hall of Fame." He was allotted a future of prophetic rank.

No wonder that Zacharias felt so overwhelmed by the fantastic nature of that news that he couldn't go along with it. Withdrawn from all human eyes, with sealed lips, he had to grow into the fulfillment which had been granted to him.

In all that touches us as so human in this Advent story, in all that is recounted about a father's and mother's joy, therefore, something else is also at work, something strange that breaks out of the framework of a touching anecdote. What is that something else?

Still another feature catches our attention. When the improbable happens and the child is born, Zacharias breaks into a song of astonished praise. But *what* does he praise? Not the child who has been given him as a long-awaited fulfillment. His song concerns another mother and another child—a child that hasn't even been born yet, a child for whom Zacharias's own son will merely prepare the way. And if the heavenly world mysteriously indicates its presence above the child John, then it will pour out all its fullness over the other child.

One last thing is to be noted. Even though the advent of that coming child still lies far over the horizon—like a constellation which has not yet come into view, but whose rising has been announced by an astronomer—Zacharias speaks of it in the past tense. "God *has* visited and redeemed his people." The time of fulfillment *has* arrived. We *are* already surrounded by the miracles of God.

What a remarkable form of advent announcement! Everywhere else in the world, where mankind waits, where it looks forward to a classless society or a world without hunger and war, or where it awaits a biologically improved human race, the talk is of vague utopias which are projected in a distant future. Here, however, the statement is not only "The future has already begun," but "It is already among us." The kingdom of God is present here and now where the miracle of Bethlehem touches us. The fulfillment of God literally changes us. It is as though scales fall from Zacharias's eyes, so that where the common observer sees only a few private exchanges in a corner of the world far removed from the hot breath of history, Zacharias discerns the great turning point of man's destiny. Not only does he hear the rustle of God's mantle above him, he also discovers that the heart of all things lies open here before him and that the New has broken in providing mankind with newness of life.

Now the events which God caused are not *completely* buried in mystery and shrouded with veils of myth. It is characteristic, rather, of the divine "style"—if I may put it that way—to work through the natural, the everyday, and the customary. God does *not* simply live and exist in a transcendent heaven high above, and the hymn "the home of the soul is up there in light" is certainly *not* correct. No, God rather comes to us, as Paul Tillich liked to say, in the "depth of being." He enters into history and is cheek-by-jowl with our daily experience. Exactly the same thing is true in this story. God appears in a quite human dimension—in the waiting and hoping of two people—and, indeed, not merely in the expectation of the messiah of Israel (which would be a religious and spiritual dimension) but in the totally human and creaturely expectation of a son, put in a consciously banal way: of a posterity.

How human that is! I believe that the Advent season arouses such homely feelings in us, not only among Christians, but also among completely secular men, because the note of waiting strikes a responsive chord in *all* our hearts. And the "humanity" of God permits us to look for his nearness in these completely human activities.

As a matter of fact our entire life is one single "waiting." As children we wait until we will become grown-ups. Or we wait for new shoes, or for our first dance. Then we wait for the end of our education, for the first self-earned money, then for our life's companion, then for children, and after that for the time when the children will be grown and on their own. So it goes, on and on.

And when we have nothing more to wait for, that is death— by no means because the end of our professional life, of all our productive functions, and ultimately our physical death await us. No, where waiting ends, that is the end of life itself.

Why is that? It is because we men always include the future in our thinking, while animals live only for the moment. Therefore my dog is not thrilled by hope for the future, nor is he vexed by anxiety for the future. That's how "human" waiting is. It is the burden, the driving force, to say nothing of the privilege of *mankind*.

But now another question: *What* are we waiting for, anyway? Is it really just the "next thing," next year's raise, the new home that we shall occupy, or the car that we are going to buy? Or do we look to what the futurologists predict for the 70's: the somewhat ominous biological interference with our environment, the miracles of laser beams, the growing automation of industry, and the ever-increasing amount of leisure time?

I believe that our waiting is not at all directed *only* toward these coming events. Our questioning eye penetrates into the future in a totally different way. In a much deeper sense, aren't we waiting for the dark and incomprehensible in our life to clear up? Aren't we waiting for the riddles which we have not yet solved to be explained? Why must some people suffer so shockingly while the rascals always land on their feet? What sense is there in a little girl falling into the hands of a fiend and being horribly mauled? Why did America become involved in Vietnam? And why must thousands of loved ones who thirsted for well-rounded life die like animals because of that involvement? How can we ever understand why people like you and me starve to death in Asia?

It is not hard to guess why we look for illumination for *that* riddle. Some sense it dimly; others know it clearly through reflection: If something blatantly senseless happens anywhere, if blind and meaningless chance rules anywhere (in just *one* spot), then our whole life is only a blind toss of the dice, a soulless interaction between energy and matter. Then there are no more "higher thoughts" that rule over us, and there is no God to "think" anything about it or to watch lovingly over our life.

No one has stated this questioning of everything so painfully and impressively as Samuel Becket in his play *Waiting for Godot*. The mysterious figure of Godot, of course, is not simply a circumlocution for God, but it most certainly is a symbol for that *X* in the background of our world which mankind must find and know if life is ever going to reveal its meaning. Therefore the two tramps Vladimir and Estragon wait for Godot. Apparently a night will fall again in which Godot fails to appear for the umpteenth time. Then everything is pointless and without sense. On stage the two men talk nothing but plain nonsense. They simply "chatter"; it all falls far short of the level of classic dialogue. What is the reason for this verbal wheel-spinning? Think for a moment. A meaningfully ordered and articulated language would obviously only make sense if that decisive figure—if Godot—really came, if one could plan further, could count on meaning, and could set up a program. If Godot doesn't come, then nothing else counts. Then the words die on one's lips; then the future is no more. Then the motor of life is disconnected and everything comes to a stop.

Sometimes I ask myself if our contemporary literature with its empty loquaciousness and its disoriented relationship to time as expressed in endless flashbacks and previews, could not be a symptom of the fact that Godot still hasn't come; and that people have given up waiting for him, that they despair of finding any meaning in life.

There is a touch of this hopelessness of waiting in vain even in Zacharias's song of praise. It too speaks of the end of hope

and of men sitting "in darkness and in the shadow of death"—
in that night where Godot never, never comes.

Does that concern us at all today? We must ask that question
honestly. Isn't it just the voice of late antiquity's pessimism
about life? Don't we modern men feel quite differently? We
enjoy life and affirm sex and cheerfully free ourselves from
outdated taboos. We plan a better, brighter world for the next
two decades. How can the shadow of death spread its chill in
such an atmosphere?

In actual fact death expresses itself for us only in coded form.
Its signals, however, cannot be ignored. We know (even in the
springtime of our lives) that we are finite, that youth passes
away, and that we had better take all we can with us because
we can't go around again. Where do young people get their
fear that they might miss something, that they might "lose
some of the action"? Don't anxieties of this sort stem from a
knowledge of the unrepeatable, onward-flowing nature of
time—from the same knowledge, therefore, that pushes us to
hurry and to use up every passing moment? "Time never says
'see you again'" is written on an old sundial, and Shakespeare
says, "O gentlemen, the time of life is short."[1]

In knowing this, it becomes apparent that we are reckoning
with the limited time allotted to us, with our finitude and with
death. The elderly woman in an old folk's home is not the only
one who does it; the teen-ager who still lives in the full bloom
of life and seems to have everything ahead of him does it too.
But the very fact that he thus has it all ahead is *itself* under a
time limit. And the time is running out; it is only a short span
of time for which the closing bell is ready to ring.

Every moment we obviously reckon with the trenchant fact
that human life is "as grass that soon withers." And the livelier
we are, the more we remember it. Precisely when we say to the
moment, as Faust did, "Linger awhile, you are so lovely"—that
is when we feel the cold breath of the shadow of death strike
us most perceptibly. For it is the fulfilled—the "lovely"—
moment that hurries by and cannot be held. No wonder that
we do not want to resign ourselves to it. No wonder that we

1. *Henry IV*, pt. 1, act 5, sc. 2.

clutch at this passing moment, that we declare money and property to be durable goods, and that we "Spin castles in the air and come farther from the goal."

Zacharias, however, sees more than this fascinatingly lovely (and therefore so melancholy) passing world. He sees a "dayspring from on high" in the midst of the shadows of death. He says that God has "visited" us in the world of death, and that we now have contact with the eternal while we are still in this transitory life. What does that mean? And what about this unusual phrase "dayspring from on high"?

If we wish to stay with this pictorial language, then the phrase obviously does not mean that this new and liberating element approaches us from the distant horizon, but that it comes to us vertically from above.

When we speak of problems that have to do with the "horizon" of our life, we generally mean the so-called ultimate questions—questions that involve the ground, goal, and meaning of our life. In such matters, philosophers like to talk about "illuminating our existence," that is, about a perspective that brings the *whole* of our life in view. The words of Zacharias, however, are silent as far as these ultimate questions, which "illuminate our existence" are concerned. One day the little child over whose cradle these words are sung will have his personal perspective on history and his own life shattered. For there will come a time in his life when the hour of despair strikes—when he becomes so confused about Christ that he tremulously asks, "Are you he that should come, or do we look for another?" In that hour all the neat explanations of history and "illuminations of his existence" that he had constructed will collapse.

In contrast to this conception, the "dayspring from on high" that Zacharias means comes vertically from above. It flows from a dimension different from that of merely human thoughts. It speaks of a blessing, a surprise and a gift which no Faustian search for meaning could find for itself.

Then what is this upsetting new element that is supposed to snatch man out of the world of death and fill him with a completely new and abiding Spirit?

Zacharias's hymn is like a Bach chorale, where each verse has a different arrangement and instrumentation and yet the *same* praise is repeated in endless variation.

The hymn testifies to God's "blessed secret" in ever-new ways. The fullness of what Zacharias is allowed to see here surpasses the power of any single word or formula to comprehend it.

It begins by saying that God is merciful to us and has turned to us with his inmost being. Luther's translation of this hymn speaks of the "heartfelt compassion" of God which meets us in the Christmas child and his forerunner. Here we are told that God has come and revealed his inmost being to us. This inmost secret of his heart is *love*.

If I should try to articulate in weak words what is said here, I might express it somewhat like this:

There are certainly some times in our life when we count on this life of ours being directed by a higher power. Christians aren't the only ones who do that. Neopagans and superstitious people also look to powers (or *a* power) that lean in the background exercising a controlling power over our life. In that situation two quite different impressions of how the world is governed come to light.

Sometimes we are thankful for a pleasure—or a lucky break. Then we are inclined to believe in a "loving God" who wishes us well, or even in favorable constellations that give us clear sailing. Another time we are faced with a streak of bad luck or we are smarting from some senseless blow of fate. Then the stars that sway our destiny seem hidden by clouds. (Myths have produced many pictures and parables of this situation.) We begin to wonder whether the divinity has a heart, in fact we doubt whether a being of this sort even exists.

This common human experience, pulling us to and fro, was also the experience of people in biblical times. Patriarchs, prophets and apostles were thankful for good times, but they nearly lost their faith when something happened that made them think the ruler of the world was senseless, unjust, or cruel. Psalm 73 contains the agonizing words, "I almost spoke as they did"—that is, as the godless for whom the mad course of this world is one continual denial, one continual compromising of God. This psalm verse is like an outcry. It is nothing less than the despairing question of how a person can believe in God and still maintain his integrity, and his intellectual honesty when the "fat cats" are permitted to flourish while decent people lose out. "This God'" cried a ship's captain recently to one of my students who was earning some money, "this God ought to come on board sometime. I'd throw him over the rail as a deckhand, because he's always bungling things. He let my best friend go to the dogs, but the real deadbeats get to enjoy life."

What is there in us that keeps us from jumping on someone when he mocks God in that self-tormenting way. Is it because we, like Zacharias, have this despairing mockery in our own hearts?

No one, not even the greatest in the kingdom of God, remains unmoved by the dark valleys of life or untouched by the anxious question of how God can permit such things—or whether there is a God at all.

Zacharias announces the one who will walk through these valleys at their darkest, and who on the cross will burst out with the dismal cry "My God, my God, why hast thou forsaken me?" And even if it is not yet possible for him to gauge the breadth of that suffering, Zacharias uses the phrase that resolves those dark secrets and contradictions; according to that phrase, the inmost secret of God is his "heartfelt compassion." That says all that can be said about his nature. With that the secret is out. There is nothing else to say after that— nothing about dark abysses, nothing demonic; he is purely and simply love.

But then is this love *also* active in something that neither we nor the disciples have ever been able to understand? Is it active in that Innocent One who must suffer and die on the gallows? We men may indeed learn the *theme* of this love, and Zacharias surely sounds it clearly in this passage, but we are not able to discern the obscure and intricate orchestration of life in which God develops this theme. Only those who grasp the defiant "Nevertheless I am continually with thee" (Ps. 73:23) of this theme will ultimately reach the point where they may see what they hardly dared to believe, confessing with Joseph, "Men intended to do evil (and they seemed to succeed at it and have the upper hand), but God intended it for good" (Gen. 50:20).

No wonder that in this song of praise Zacharias not only looks forward to a future fulfillment in which this love of God will overwhelmingly reveal itself, but that he also goes back to the time of the fathers, remembering the words that God "spoke through the mouth of his holy prophets," and the covenant that he made with the fathers, and thus recalling the obscure and intricate history that this love produced long before *we* came on the scene. They were all men who had to struggle with the same obscurities we face: like Abraham they were called out from friends and fatherland and sent into the unknown; like Job they experienced horrors over which no fatherly countenance shed its light; like Jeremiah they suffered through dark spots in history from which God seemed to withdraw, remaining silent and arousing suspicions that he was dead.

If we listen to the great witnesses of the Bible to whom Zacharias refers here, we certainly do not meet people who bear the stamp of fascinating experiences—experiences which we typically do *not* have. They are not people who have a glorious conviction and self-certainty which are beyond our reach today. On the contrary, we see simple men who cry out of the depths (as we do), who were hemmed in by circumstances that seemed to raise questions about God (as we do) and yet who in pain and inexpressible confidence won through to certainty in that covenant which God had promised them and to the "heartfelt compassion" that served as a guiding star to them when they were surrounded by the darkness of life.

It is an indescribable comfort to be a part of this company— not among heroes of the spirit or of faith who are above all earthly need (as though there really were such people!) but among people like you and me who must despair if God does not again and again surround them with his peace; not among saints and showy examples of morality, but among weak and defeated men who are nevertheless set back on their feet time and again. For they trust the assurance that their sins are forgiven and that neither death nor life, neither things present nor things to come can separate them from the love of God.

Now do we understand what Zacharias meant when he said that now we can serve God without fear as long as we live? "Without fear"—that is like a prophecy of the gospel of Christmas night when the fear-stunned shepherds were told, "Fear not." This word is not directed to men who may be too dull to be frightened, but to men who are really worried. Perhaps they have a lively imagination and the gift of "putting two and two together." That's why they see things that frighten them. In this text Zacharias does not promise us that these psychic mortgages will be lifted from us. No indeed! The anxiety-producing material continues to flow in our blood-stream. But we hear the cry, "Fear not." And therefore we know that someone is there to see us through the darkness—but not only to see us through. No, he is master of the darkness, able to command the waves and calm the storm when it suits his purpose.

Zacharias indicates that, too, although by means of an obscure figure of speech when he says that God has "raised up a horn of salvation for us." That is to say that he is not only a God of love who sympathetically stands by his children in their distress. He also has the power to change things. He not only hears our cries from the depths; he also draws us out of the depths and "he will do things that will surprise us."

The horn symbol alludes to the eighth chapter of Daniel and to other parts of the Old Testament. These horns are typically symbols of bestiality, of wild fury and blind force. Horns often appear as somewhat sinister symbols on the national coats of arms where they exude anything but salvation. The devil himself is frequently depicted with horns.

But now, when God keeps his advent, the horn of *salvation* is raised. Now a counterforce is on the field, a match for the sinister powers. And even the great of this world, from Nebuchadnezzar to Mao Tse-tung cannot upset God. They lull themselves with the illusion that men make history and that their horn is the battering ram with which they can shake the world's timbers, yet in reality they themselves are part of God's plan and must serve his ends whether they know it or not and whether they like it or not. The heartfelt compassion of God swings like a bell over our dark world, and its theme prevails despite the riddles of our history and even despite everything of human origin that resists it and poses as Lord of the present.

The lordship of this "horn" therefore brings freedom from fear. Even when prison walls surround us, when cancer threatens us, or someone gravely disappoints us we can say with Bonhoeffer:

> While all the powers of good aid and attend us,
> boldly we'll face the future, come what may.
> At even and at morn God will befriend us,
> and oh, most surely on each newborn day![2]

In saying that, I also note one last question that may affect many people. They could voice it in the painful cry, "I get the message, but I don't have the faith." I still grapple with my problems, I have my times of depression, and I may see myself as a speck of that darkness which the "shadow of death" spreads around us all. How can *I* get to the point where that hopeful waiting of Advent sheds its brilliance around me? How can *I* get a bit of that peace that Zacharias praises so highly? If I cannot share in this joy of fulfillment, then it's "weary, stale, flat, and unprofitable."[3] That's my question.

A few years ago someone told a friend of mine, "I can't believe since the war. I saw too much. But I survive because I know that there are people who can believe." In other words, he looked to proxies who could pray, those who were given the confidence that he himself was apparently denied.

I myself have known some people who did not practice a faith of their own but who nevertheless didn't want to live without those who did. It's almost like a piggyback ride. A person can't travel under his own spiritual steam and hitch-

2. Dietrich Bonhoeffer, *Letters and Papers from Prison*, enlarged edition, trans. Reginald Fuller, Frank Clarke and others (SCM Press and Macmillan, 1971), p. 401.
3. *Hamlet*, act 1, sc. 2.

hikes, so to speak, with others, living off what they receive. It is a sort of refined free-loading. That type of faith is certainly very immature, almost infantile, and hardly deserves the name. And yet there are moments when all of us, even the so-called confessing Christians, are burned out and empty, when we "feel nothing of his might," and when black nothingness pulls us down like a whirlpool. Then edifying thoughts are farthest from our minds and even our prayers tire out before they reach the ceiling. That is the time when it becomes important to us that *others* believe and compare prayers so we can slip in on one that we find printed somewhere. That is the time for "piggyback faith."

Isn't that why we repeat the Lord's Prayer, because it originated with someone who was nearer to God than we will ever get? Or we read a hymn, perhaps Paul Gerhardt's "Put thou thy trust in God." We read it when we are really down or in a corner, without a trace of our own strength, letting Paul Gerhardt's faith carry us. And isn't that exactly what Zacharias did when he went down the list of great believers who had known the glory of God? Wasn't he too sometimes gagged by pure hopelessness?

Perhaps that is our last resort when the dark clouds over-whelm us—that there is a congregation that thanks and praises God, lifting its hands on my behalf when I myself cannot utter a sound or lie sick or dying, no longer master of my words and thoughts.

Jesus Christ lives all around us in his witnesses; their doxology may not cease, even though individual hearts are dead and lips sealed. Between me and every shadow stands Jesus Christ, and there is no darkness with which that light cannot deal. Zacharias's hymn testifies to that dawn.

13. WHEN NOTHING MAKES SENSE

Now when John heard in prison about the deeds of the Christ, he sent word by his disciples and said to him, "Are you he who is to come, or shall we look for another?"

And Jesus answered them, "Go and tell John what you hear and see: the blind receive their sight and the lame walk, lepers are cleansed and the deaf hear, and the dead are raised up, and the poor have good news preached to them.

"And blessed is he who takes no offense at me."

Matthew 11:2–6

Sometimes we tell ourselves, "It can't keep on this way." Or perhaps when we sit at our regular table with a group of old friends and the conversation is in full swing we say: "Things can't possibly stay like this. Hard times will certainly come again, when the beneficiaries of our rising economy will no longer indulge in orgies of buying at Christmastime, but will once again be thankful for a crust of bread. Even in politics everything must change. Instead of many nations and hostile hemispheres there must be a world-state. In place of unjust and exploitative structures there must rise a society which guarantees everyone an equal chance and which will not let monopolies emerge. Then, at one blow, human misery would end. In short, the whole world must be brought into line."

The demands and wishes I have expressed in somewhat worldly language, and with sharpened relevance, were what John the Baptist also said in his day, in his fashion, and from his perspective. Of course, he wasn't sitting in a restaurant bantering with friends, where the talk can get pretty loose. He spoke from the barren wilderness. And it wasn't just nighttime conversation for him; he said it with the deadly earnestness of a messenger who has been entrusted with the fateful news: "The world as it now is will end. The axe is laid to the roots of the trees. He whose hand will wield that axe shall follow me.

He will no longer concern himself with such paltry things as my baptizing in the Jordan. He comes with spirit and with fire first to destroy and then to let a new world arise out of the flames. Therefore halt on your downward path! For God's sake—that is a warning—turn back so that you may be fit for the moment when the new world comes. Otherwise you will be destroyed in a judgment that will make Noah's flood look like child's play."

Those were great and almost wild words; they told of nothing less than a cataclysmic judgment: God would shake the framework of the world with his own hands, commissioning a looming messianic figure to plow up the old, rotten world and to bring a new one to light.

Now, in Jesus of Nazareth, this looming messianic figure was finally on the scene. But the anticipated catastrophe did not occur—or at least it looked disturbingly different—because it was John himself over whom the catastrophe broke. He sat imprisoned in some dank hole. And the sadder and viler it got, the more intensely he picked up every report from outside that came to him: When would the anticipated overthrow finally arrive? When would the foundations of the earth shake because the man from Nazareth had given the word—had *finally* given the word?

Yet the storm did not break. The world ran along its old tracks. The flowers bloomed and the children played in the streets as though nothing would happen. And so John sank deeper into his thoughts: Was he perhaps to languish here until he came to the end of both his life and his illusions?

I believe that all of us have experienced this sort of disconsolate musing. We sometimes envision how our life should turn out, or how *God* should make it turn out if he is really God. But then something completely different happens. A job that suited us to a "T" goes to someone else; the cure for a disease is denied us. In the process we had secretly set up a chance for God to prove that he was the director of our life. But he didn't take advantage of the opportunity. Cancer and multiple sclerosis ran their natural course without any intervention from him.

Moreover, we not only entertain quite definite expectations as far as God is concerned, but also in respect to persons with whom we come in contact each day. For example, we divide the people we meet into quite definite types, and we think we know how they will behave in certain cases. This one is a typical status-seeker, that one is a bundle of nerves, and that one over there is a faithful soul who wouldn't hurt a fly. Unwittingly we have a pigeonhole, or better, a whole host of pigeonholes on hand into which we put people. These pigeonholes seem to tell us exactly what we can expect from this or that person. That is why we are surprised again and again when they *don't* fit into such a scheme and when they do something shocking for which we are not prepared. Take, for example, Hitler or Mao Tse-tung. When a dictator like that pats a child on the head, we say, "Well, he's not so bad after all." If he is cruel and orders mass executions, we state with surprise, "He's a lot worse than we thought." We even have a pigeonhole like that prepared for God.

But woe be it if God doesn't fit what we have expected of him—if he thus acts differently from what he ought to do! Then we immediately threaten him by saying that we don't think he exists. "For," as Martin Walser rightly said in his novel *Halftime*, "my God is put together out of distinct plans that I have made with myself." No wonder, then, that I abandon him and let him go when he doesn't operate "according to plan." (Was it really God who failed, or have my plans merely turned out to be trash? Yet I seldom ask myself this question.)

John too is committed to such plans and postulates. He is a man exactly like you and me. Jesus of Nazareth, he estimates, is to be the great world-renewer. But he does nothing beyond giving a few persons "new hearts," and he thus contents himself with the inner man. But no fire falls from heaven to incinerate the scoundrels and rebels; no mass conversion sets in. God persistently wraps himself in silence and lets everything go along at the same old pace. *How are we supposed to believe then?*

Doesn't this musing, heretical, protesting John live again

among us and in us? Isn't his voice in our own querulous thoughts? For example, what changes in the world have two thousand years of Christianity brought? Isn't there still suffering and sinning, loving and killing, just as there always was? Has even *one* war been avoided, *one* prison become superfluous, or even *one* nation become a truly just state because Jesus Christ existed? Is he then really the one for whom the world waited as for a fulfillment? Or must we look for some other men and other miracles—the classless society, perhaps, or the twenty-hour week, or 1984? Is Jesus Christ, instead of the fulfillment of our life, perhaps only an interlude, an intermezzo in history—touching and awe-inspiring in his life, granted!— but still only an intermezzo that helps no one in South Vietnam or behind the wall in Berlin.

Granted, one may discuss such questions. It can be done, for instance, under the title "the absoluteness of Christianity" or also under the general question of whether Christ was *more* than anyone else who bore our human frame—if he was, for example, the "Son of God."

John, however, did not open a discussion. His question, "Are you the Christ?" arose neither out of curiosity nor out of interest in the philosophy of religion. When one sits in a prison cell waiting for the executioner, one can no longer afford the comfort of intellectual curiosity. Then the step outside in the corridor, the jingle of a bunch of keys, is more real than any "problem." For steps and keys can mean someone is coming for me. In such situations only *basic* questions remain, questions that involve my being or nonbeing. This question, however— whether Jesus is not an illusion and whether his messenger, the imprisoned John, is not a cheated cheater—this question *is* basic and cuts pretty deep. It is "existential." For my personal future depends on how this question is to be answered. If this Nazarene has the power to shake the foundations of the world in God's name, then he must ultimately be able also to destroy the prison walls behind which his witness languishes. Of course, the opposite is also true: If he lets his witness, his best friend, fall prey to the executioner's blade, without being able to halt the mills of this shameful justice, then that is a flagrant contradiction of all the claims he ever made. That is the bankruptcy of all the hopes that ever were pinned on him! Thus, here in the prison cell all questions become a few degrees hotter, heavier, and more portentous.

Yet the mental crisis of John reaches still deeper regions than that of mere self-preservation. Wouldn't the witnesses of ancient times, wouldn't Moses and the prophets and the other men of God likewise have believed and hoped in vain—*if* this messiah is only a bubble? In that case wouldn't everything that he had formerly held sacred as the faith of the fathers and as pious tradition fall apart? "I would gladly die in this hole," John the Baptist may have said to himself, "if only the faith that still supports me in this darkness wouldn't die with me. My head may roll, but at least let my heart not freeze when it discovers nothing but emptiness around it! Let me find one little tiny spark of meaning and hope remaining."

Really, the question, "Are you the one whose coming was promised to us?" is not a question of curiosity; it is posed by anyone who feels the earth shake beneath his feet while his heart shrinks from the ugly face of meaninglessness.

Nevertheless, a quite different tone is also audible in that despairing question that the couriers bring. It is an unheard-of tone, so to speak, that arises from areas where despair can no longer have any power over it. Even though John cannot understand his Master's way, he has not simply given him up yet, instead he brings the despair to Jesus. From a "psychological" point of view a quite different reaction would be much more plausible to us. We would expect that John in his musing would have said to himself, "I am bankrupt; I've made a mistake; it's all over. Others are welcome to hope in other saviors and experience the same failure. I, at any rate, am completely cured of all hopes that someone will grasp the wheel of world history and force it into a new course. And now that I am stripped of everything and have nothing to hold on to, I will at least die with dignity—like the soldier of Pompeii who was standing his meaningless watch when the lava rolled over him and choked him."

But that is precisely what doesn't happen! John does not

call out his question into dark, empty space; he poses it to Jesus himself. Notice that he doesn't ask if *he* is indeed the one whose coming was promised. He asks, "Are *you* the one whose coming was promised?" Here is what might be called a "despairing confidence" in Jesus: *he* will know and *he* will certainly tell John.

It is noteworthy that John does not demand a "proof." Proofs are usually desired when one is suspicious. If someone must establish an alibi, for example, it is because he is definitely mistrusted and is suspected of a criminal act. John, however, demands no "proof" from his master. He isn't suspicious; he obviously trusts him. If Jesus should reply, "Don't worry, John, I *am* the one for whom you have been waiting," then John would be satisfied. Then he really throws himself upon Jesus with despairing confidence. And he therefore addresses Jesus personally, turning directly to him. The *one* word that this Nazarene will now speak suffices for him. That is the extent to which, despite all skeptical brooding, his confidence in this Nazarene and his integrity remains unbroken.

It may be somewhat startling when I dare to add the following observation: By the question which thus struggled to the surface in that cell on death row, John came closer to the secret than in the greatest moments of his "public career." Nearer even than in those moments when the crowds hung spellbound on every word, and he seemed to be the ambassador plenipotentiary of God Almighty.

By directing his despairing question to Jesus himself, he did (in a premonitory and certainly unconscious way) what the Lord himself would do in a still darker hour on Golgotha—in an hour when his weakness on the cross seemed to mock every hope that anyone had placed in him. In that moment the power of despair and nothingness broke over the crucified and he cried, "My God, my God, why hast thou forsaken me?" That cry in the night of Golgotha is like a declination of the message of John.

If I may put the similarity of the two despairing cries somewhat sharply, I would give the cry of the crucified the following form: "My God, my God, am *I* really the one who should come? *If* I were really the one, should it have happened like this—that I fall into the hands of men? Should death be stronger than I—I who have awakened the dead? Must you not then, my Father, declare yourself to me? Must you not let me climb down from my cross as you shatter the night around me with your lightning?" The Master will be banished to still more terrifying abysses of nothingness than his doubt-plagued disciple in the prison cell.

Yet the deeper relationship of both cries of despair lies elsewhere. For Jesus Christ does not simply cry out his need into the night of Golgotha either. It is typical that he does not cry "Where is God? Where is everything I built on and held to—why is it holding back?" Instead he tells his Father himself what it is that clutches at his heart. He doesn't talk "about" God (as one would about an unknown *X* that melts away completely into nothingness); he says "thou" to his Father; he says, "my God." He doesn't complain to an unknown; he casts himself on his Father's heart. At the moment, indeed, he no longer understands the decision of that heart. But he trusts that that heart beats for him nevertheless. And therefore he is really not forsaken, but remains in contact with the Father.

There is an unbelievable parallel to all this in James Baldwin's novel *Another Country*. It is so crass and horrible that one hesitates to cite it in connection with such a discussion. But even so, I will do it. After a bungled life in which God melted away into nothingness for him, and even his fellow men faded into insubstantial shadows, the young Negro, Rufus, jumps off a bridge in New York. But before he commits suicide, one last thought flashes through him: "You wretch," he says to the lost God, "you puking almighty wretch, am I not your child too? Now I'm coming to you!" And then he leaps into the water. That really doesn't sound edifying. But is it really only the blasphemy of a so-called atheist? Didn't he too—horribly wrapped in a curse and cramped by a clenched fist—still say "you" to God? Wasn't he a despairing child who wanted to throw himself into the eternal arms? As long as I can still say "my Father" or even "your child is coming to you," I have not been forsaken. That is why what sounded like the inarticulate cry of a desperate man on Golgotha ended in the words of a deep peace: "Father, into thy hands I commit my spirit" (Luke 23:46).

In exactly the same way, a margin of peace surrounds the despair of John. For he is clear about one thing: that Jesus of Nazareth *alone* knows ultimately who he is. He is so great that I can entrust myself and my doubt to him, and to him alone. And even though for the moment John no longer knows whether this Jesus is really the last, the "Son of God," yet he does know that this figure of his Master is greater than his own heart and that there is shelter in him.

And now comes the sudden, dramatic turn of events. The one who has been thus addressed now answers, "Go and tell John," he charges the couriers, "what you hear and see: the blind receive their sight and the lame walk, lepers are cleansed and the deaf hear, and the dead are raised up, and the poor have good news preached to them." The first thing worth noting about this message appears to be that the Lord does not get himself involved in theoretical discussion about whether he, Jesus Christ, is a unique figure of history, representing the so-called absoluteness of Christianity. Jesus hardly once, maybe never, said who he was directly and in unambiguous form. When he speaks about the mystery of his person, he talks in an oblique fashion, he withdraws, so to speak, into indirect lighting, and lets the people guess more and become more puzzled than if he said something "dogmatic" about himself. He even played "hard to get" sometimes and chose what amounted to the indirect Socratic method.

That is what he does here. He does not tell the messengers, "Of course I *am* the one who should come, and you don't need to wait for anyone else!" Instead he answers, "See for yourselves what is going on around you! Look at the lame, the blind, and the guilt-ridden! Elsewhere everything goes its logical way, pressing on to unavoidable consequences: sickness is followed by death, death by decay, and after guilt comes punishment. See for yourselves how I intervene in this cycle's mechanism of events and create the New, how transformations occur around me."

He speaks of himself in this indirect way. One can recognize the secret of his person only in the reflection, as it were, of what happens around him. That's all he says. Then he refers the questioner to that reflection.

Then what image of the Lord *does* become visible in that reflection? That is the next question.

Certainly it is not the image of a world revolutionary that John had constructed for him. He didn't lift the world off its hinges at all, in fact he himself said that the world would run on as before right up to the last judgment. People will marry and be given in marriage. They will shout to high heaven and die of grief, there will be suffering and death, and even the furies of war and the hoofbeats of the apocalyptic horsemen will resound over the earth "until he comes." Then he will not actually "transform" the world; he intends to be our Savior in the midst of this world.

Yet *how* will he save us if everything goes on as it is? That is still the problem. Let me sharpen the realism of the question even more: How do *I* notice something of this salvation if my conscience, say, accuses me (perhaps because I have destroyed the life of another person), if I suffer under my unfaithfulness, if I succumb to the superiority of my senses, if my uneasy spirit will not let me sleep, and if there are specific questions, anxieties, and passions in my life which I cannot get rid of—not at all? Once again, how do I tell then that Jesus is intervening in my life, that something new is happening and that the switches of my life have been thrown? How do I tell that? What good to me are the old miracle stories to which the message alludes? Even assuming for the moment that these miracles really happened, what have these occasional, individual, mighty works accomplished? The young man from Nain may well have risen from his coffin. But ultimately death came for him anyway. And the poor that Jesus comforted still became sorrowful again later on. What, then, did a few drops of miraculous help accomplish in the bucket of human misery? Ultimately the torturing and killing will continue in Vietnam, in India people will go on starving as before, and in our own country we still dance heedlessly on the volcano.

It is entirely proper that we vent our doubt in this way. For one thing is sure: Jesus himself does not waver when our faith begins to totter. Of course it all depends on our confession of doubt not being cynical (even the Negro Rufus was not cynical, despite his blasphemous phraseology); we must come as injured men seeking the physician. And if we bear our doubt to Jesus himself, then we are *not* cynical.

And what, then, does he reply to the messengers? What does he want John to understand when he refers to the revolutionary, cheering transformations that take place around him in the sick, the poor, and the dead? He wants to tell him this: "I don't hold lectures for you on the loving God, nor do I bring any philosophy about human existence. But wherever my word is heard (no matter whether it is 'blessed' or 'woe') something *happens* and nothing remains as it was. The sick become well, the unfortunate are marvelously comforted, and wounded consciences are healed. Lectures can teach a person, but they don't heal anyone."

In fact everyone who has known Jesus Christ will testify: "Since that time something new has entered my life. The darkness in my life that used to throw me into despondency can master me no longer. Granted, I have cares—as others do. Yet daily I experience the miracle of having someone who will lift them from me, someone to whom I can entrust them. And if his hand touches them, they are mysteriously transformed. Before, they were an oppressive mortgage on my life, yet now they have become the opportunity for faith. They have become the material out of which God will fashion my hope and a joyful 'nevertheless.' And when I discover that my end is at hand, that I am becoming old and weary, he will transform the sorrow of departure into the joy of homecoming."

No one leaves Christ as he came to him. Everything is transformed. There is a new air about everything. What was formerly inedible stone is transformed into bread. My anxieties become the raw material for a new hope. And what previously was the burden of my life I now no lonegr need to bear; it is, to quote the neat phrase of Rudolf Alexander Schröder, exactly reversed: "The burden bears me."

He is the great transformer. Of course, that cannot be seen in advance, nor can it be observed from outside. You must try him once. You can experience it only in the doing and in the risk of discipleship. You experience it only through involvement.

That, therefore, is the message of those miracles and transformations: You may bring me everything that worries you, not only the wounds in your heart and your tormenting skepticism, but also your physical pains and your toothache, your cares about education and your love problems, and even the examination that you must take in the morning. For "nothing can happen to me that he has not examined and blessed to my use." Everything must go through him before it hits me. And *if* it then hits me (and of course he never promised that his redeemed would be carried smoothly across all abysses like some sort of fair-haired lad), *if* it then hits me I at least know that it has passed his inspection and gotten his "O.K." Then, when I am exhilarated by great gain or depressed by worries, I receive it with his greetings, and my joys are doubled while my pain is cut in half. Isn't it true that whether something is tough or easy in my life depends ultimately on one thing: whether I can receive it from his hand or not? If I only see a dark, anonymous fate as the sender of everything that hits me, then it all becomes anxious, comfortless and hopeless. If, however, I see his greetings on my way, then I always receive a positive order; then I know that it is not in vain, that it must serve my best interests, and that it will be creative. Then I know that his higher thoughts have already prepared the goal for me, while I, with my human thoughts, am still groping in the dark.

Is all of that an answer to John or is it not? Certainly it is a very indirect answer, since John himself must speak the last word. It depends on him whether this message will display the lordship of Jesus to him or not.

For Jesus is always, before everything else, the *questioner*. And if I intend to be true to the text I must let this tone of "questioning" ring out at this point. It is the same question that faces those who hear or read these words. For he certainly does not want to impose any dogma upon us; he wants to reach our hearts. He wants our hearts to be questioned and questioning—and restless in both. For he has called the hungry and thirsty, but never the satisfied, blessed.

Therefore he closes his message to John with the warning, "And blessed is he who takes no offense at me." To whom, then, is he offensive, who is annoyed with him?

Annoyance and fierce disappointment always arise when one wants, as a nonparticipant and therefore from outside—at a "theoretical distance"—to find out if Jesus Christ is the One and Only. One lets the world of religions, so to speak, pass in review, looking at the Moslems and the Buddhists or even Radhakrishnan and the Marxists, in order to pick out a suitable one. *As if that would work!* Clarity about Jesus of Nazareth can only be achieved through *involvement*, only by betting on him—perhaps by helping a person with whom I really have no natural ties, but whom I am ready to recognize as my brother in the name of Jesus. We must at least associate with him if we want to know what there is to him.

If a child tells his mother, "You are the most beautiful mother in the world; you are the only mother who ever was," he has not reached this conclusion by having all the mothers in the world pass by in review so that he can test which of them is the most beautiful and the best. The child, *without* having arranged that comparison, is bound to this one mother in love, looks to her in confidence, and risks himself and all that he is and has and longs for in the way of security on this one and only person whom he loves above all else. That is a paltry and thoroughly inadequate image of how we can also come to say to Jesus, "You are my only comfort in life and death. You are the first and the last, the Alpha and Omega; and you are the one and only person for whom we could wait."

14. HOW DO I OVERCOME LIFE'S BOREDOM AND ANXIETY?

On the last day of the feast, the great day, Jesus stood up and proclaimed, "If any one thirst, let him come to me and drink. He who believes in me, as the scripture has said, 'Out of his heart shall flow rivers of living water.'" Now this he said about the Spirit, which those who believed in him were to receive; for as yet the Spirit had not been given, because Jesus was not yet glorified.

When they heard these words, some of the people said, "This is really the prophet." Others said, "This is the Christ." But some said, "Is the Christ to come from Galilee? Has not the scripture said that the Christ is descended from David, and comes from Bethlehem, the village where David was?"

So there was a division among the people over him. Some of them wanted to arrest him, but no one laid hands on him.

The officers then went back to the chief priests and Pharisees, who said to them, "Why did you not bring him?" The officers answered, "No man ever spoke like this man!"

The Pharisees answered them, "Are you led astray, you also? Have any of the authorities or of the Pharisees believed in him? But this crowd, who do not know the law, are accursed."

Nicodemus, who had gone to him before, and who was one of them, said to them, "Does our law judge a man without first giving him a hearing and learning what he does?"

They replied, "Are you from Galilee too? Search and you will see that no prophet is to rise from Galilee."

John 7:37–52

This story is full of dramatic movement. It is about thirsty people and people dying of thirst who are suddenly offered a spring. Those who have not yet been in such a situation can, for instance, read in Hans Bertram's *Flight into Hell* what it means when a pilot must make an emergency landing in the desert and look for traces of water in a barren land hostile to life.

Another part of our story also presents similar tension. I refer

194

to the puzzling question of the person of Jesus. Obscurely, the people detect something: The solution to everything that I struggle with so hopelessly could lie in what this man says. His speech echoes with a tone that is unheard of, that has never before been perceived. Yet remarkably, this impression of the unheard of is immediately knocked in the head by putting Jesus of Nazareth into "historical" and "geographical" co-ordinates, and thereby pigeonholing him. "Nothing new from the north," they tell themselves, thinking of his provincial origin in Nazareth. He too is only "human." How is *he* to put my life in a new dimension when he, after all, couldn't manage his own life, but lost it. So they told themselves, trying to still the vibrations that his words sent thrilling through them.

The story, which began so dramatically, soon disappears into the sand. As the curtain falls, one goes home and promptly forgets it. What appeared exciting for a moment ends in the boredom of everydayness.

Why is it, anyway, that countless people give a faint yawn to the black book in which Christianity, oddly enough, seeks for nothing less than life itself? But there are many times when those of us, too, who do force ourselves to read it in the morning or at the close of the day, have to push ourselves a little when we want to effect that transition from the television screen or the newspaper to that black book. Dorothy Sayers, who has written a number of excellent and exciting detective stories, she of all people, at least experienced the Bible in a totally different way. She once said, "The Christian faith is the most exciting drama that has ever been offered to the human imagination." And in another passage, "Those who saw the risen Christ became and remained convinced that life was worth living and that death is null and void: a very different attitude from that of the modern defeatists who are so convinced that life is a misfortune and that death—a little illogically—is a still greater catastrophe." Dorothy Sayers means that something so ele-mental, so aggressive happens here that it makes you catch your breath once you have discovered it. In any case, this is the opposite of all boredom.

Why is it, then, that despite all these discoveries Christianity still is frequently boring? Why is it that this deadly boredom threatens to cover everything that goes on in the church with mildew and neutralize it?

I believe the answer lies in *one* fact: that we no longer expect that God could really break into our lives in a revolutionary way, that he could really turn my now-burdensome marriage inside out, or could actually transform me from a wet blanket into a person who affirms and accepts life. We no longer dare to expect that he can take our secret anxiety from us as we face the possibility of a devaluation of currency or an escalation in domestic politics or in the Near and Far Eastern theaters of war. We dare not believe that he will manage it so that I can go joyfully into the future, awaiting the coming day with its miracles and its surprises. Instead of that, God has become merely a ceremonial laurel tree on marriage altars and coffins. Outside of that he is a comfort which the aged substitute for real joys that are no longer within their powers.

Boredom apparently comes from the fact that we human beings have taken our lives into our own hands, intending that no one, certainly not God, should help us. Thus we have stopped speaking and reckoning with him in a natural and realistic way. Instead, we drown in a lonely monologue with ourselves. Jean-Paul Sartre once described hell in this sense as a place where one was "by himself."

For many of our contemporaries, technology and space travel have become a sort of symbol, telling us that it is especially fine and even exhilarating that man has thus taken his life into his own hands, that he himself now conducts things from the world's podium, and that there is nothing beyond what he has brought into being through technology or organization. Mankind has achieved the status of majority stockholder in the firm "Creation, Inc." He has added an eighth day to the seven days of creation, and the new one is under his administration and responsibility. He has far surpassed and will surpass still farther what God brought into being at the paltry start of things when the world began. The "old man," the boss, is deposed, and his residence, called heaven, is declared a part of man's domain. We in the West are perhaps a bit more cautious and let the boss still halfway count for something. We too think exactly the same way about man's majority stock holdings but we tell ourselves, "The old man founded the firm and we still celebrate his anniversaries. We have marked our date-books for formal calls on Christmas and Easter." No wonder that Christianity tastes so flat and dull. Anniversary contacts are never very attractive.

And now this story tells us that Jesus Christ has to do with our thirst and our drinking. This concerns the most elemental level of our life. He has to do with those things I can in no case avoid, those things that involve my natural drive for self-preservation. I can dispense with mental and musical enjoyments if I have to. During the war we all had to do that, and it was possible to a certain extent. For a time I can get along without caviar, and in a pinch without daily bread. But even a man on a hunger strike must drink. There is no such thing as a thirst-strike. Jesus' involvement with our life is just that primitive, that elemental. "If anyone thirst, let him come to me and drink. If one believes in me, as the Scripture says, then the water of life will well up in his being and pour forth in streams."

For what do we really thirst? We must start off by recognizing that this question is an open one. There is not one word to indicate that mankind thirsts for God or for religion or for heaven. Perhaps we ourselves would be hard put to it to tell what it is that we need. Only *that* you are driven toward some goal or other and that you are still far from this fulfillment of your longing—that you know. Perhaps your situation is similar to that of some of Wilhelm Raske's characters, who also have a great hunger but cannot precisely state what it is that they crave.

It is indeed paradoxical that in precisely this situation, the feast of tabernacles, Jesus calls for thirsty men. For this was a feast where people milled around in crowds, with food stalls, refreshment tents, and all sorts of side shows (if we can update the case a little). Granted, before this traditional vintage and harvest festival moved into its more frolicsome phase, the people did something that we today don't usually do at such carnivals. They went into the temple as pilgrims. Moreover, they came from great distances, with bag and baggage, afoot and with considerable effort, at least they didn't ride in upholstered sight-seeing buses. There they called to mind the mighty works in their history; they gave praise and thanks for miraculous deliverance from bondage, and for gracious refreshment through the thirsty stretches of the wilderness. But this pious center of the festival was wreathed by the joy of popular merry-making. The celebration of the wine harvest raised the pitch to a high point. People had saved all year for the accompanying hilarity, and now they felt inwardly and outwardly full.

When Jesus now calls out for the thirsty on the last and climactic day of a festival like that, one could almost suppose that he had made a slight mistake in his choice of times. For the people *have* all quenched their thirst. Their religious obligations are discharged and even their dry throats are lubricated.

But is it really the wrong time? Jesus Christ sees more deeply. He knows that precisely when men have reached their goal and when they outwardly appear to be satisfied, then they detect more strongly than at any other time that a great emptiness surrounds them, and that they may have been building castles in the air while they drifted farther away from their goal. "And no matter if one drinks till he is tipsy, he will never wash down the bitterness," says Erich Kästner in the *Lyrical Medicine Chest*. Today, when things are once again going well for many people economically, and the living standard is fairly good, don't our hearts echo with the question of whether this is really supposed to be the content of our life: to have enough to live on and to enjoy ice-cold drinks while watching television? In the Scandinavian welfare states the suicide rate for youth has climbed to a dizzying height. It is not love trouble or fear of punishment that drives them to death; it is boredom, it is fear of the spinning wheels of a mechanical life that runs well oiled and expertly tended, but doesn't drive anything anymore. Shortly before his death, Boris Pasternak said to one of his visitors, "Man sought his security in money, in possessions, in capital goods. . . . In the era of world wars, in the atomic age, however, capital goods don't mean the same thing. . . . We have learned we are in essence simply guests, travelers between two stations." Isn't it the same with many of us who are more or less satiated? Wouldn't we like to declare ourselves void in some suit, but just don't know which one? Don't we thirst for something without knowing what? Don't we find ourselves on a journey without knowing the name of our station? Ionesco says in his *Diaries:* "The human comedy doesn't attract me enough. I am not entirely of this world. . . . I am from elsewhere. And it is worth finding this elsewhere beyond the walls. But where is it?"

Jesus Christ knows why he chose the moment of satiety to pose the question about thirst. For the people assembled here *are* thirsty, and the Bible is full of allusions to that: They suffer under the test that God permits unrighteousness in the world, that the godless are "fat and sassy," enjoying their good fortune, while the "ever true and faithful" ones carry on a losing business. They suffer under the great silence of God, who lets all that go on without intervening. *That*, therefore, is their great thirst: to have to suffer in this dried-out world without at least hearing the springs of God bubbling a bit in their direction. *That* is their great thirst: to bear within themselves the consuming desire that the distant God might become detectable just *once*—might come close enough for us to say, "That was him; there he made himself known." Thirst is just another word for hope that torments itself and threatens to confuse itself. The pious folk in Israel, who thus hungered and thirsted for righteousness, had one additional characteristic: They refused to quench their thirst with substitutes—with ideologies, utopias, and false gods; with golden calves or even with the drugs of indifference. They endured their thirst. They held fast to the divine promise that one day, one day the hour would come when God would show himself in his majesty. And now Jesus lets them know that the hour of fulfillment has arrived. He himself is the event in which God comes among us.

Naturally one immediately asks himself *how* that is possible and *if* it is possible—or could it just be some shaky dogma that is asserted here? Isn't the opposite more likely? Doesn't God's disguise become most impenetrable precisely in the fate of Jesus of Nazareth, instead of letting the mask fall so that finally, finally we could see God face to face? Is Jesus not a man who must taste suffering and death as we all do? Didn't the gates of heaven remain shut over his cross, so that he burst out with a last cry of forsakenness? Is *he* then the one to quench our thirst—that thirst that God might finally put in a tangible and obvious appearance so that we would know where we stood with him, whether we could live with him or whether he was only an opiate for the people?

Then is the satisfaction of our thirst to be in him? How can that happen?

If anyone watches this Savior, and sees how he lives in eternal conversation with the Father and comes out of his peace, if he sees how close he is to those in despair, how he goes to the unclean and the outcasts and lays his hand on the heads of children, that person has taken a look into the heart of the Father himself and now is able to endure life. Its riddles and torments can no longer get the better of him, because he has seen the hand that holds him—that hand that will indeed not spare him from the abysses, but will support him in every depth, that will bring him back every time he runs away and will give his uneasy conscience peace.

And our text contains yet another mysterious suggestion: The thirst will be quenched when the Spirit of God performs his work among men and when it turns out that Jesus Christ is the event that makes that happen. What is meant by this suggestion? Some people may see it as a mystic oracle. I would like to take what this passage means by "Spirit" and bring it into connection with life situations that are familiar to us.

We have all had the experience of being in a state of despair. Perhaps a nagging guilt robbed us of sleep. Perhaps a person whom we did not think we could live without threatened to leave us. Or we faced an operation. Or we didn't know how we would pay our debts. We looked for a comforting and supportive word. And as we thus rummaged around in our memory, a few little phrases that we had learned in church school came to mind.

"My thoughts are not your thoughts." "In all things God works for good with those who love him." "Be not anxious for tomorrow." But the remarkable thing was that these words had no power; they lay like dead stones in our hand, so that we finally threw them away again in disappointment. When someone gives up his spirit, he becomes cold and dead. These words seem to have given up their spirit and to be without any hint of life. Therefore they became word-corpses, and we couldn't get anywhere with them.

But where Jesus Christ is, *these* dead also arise. There the dead words have spirit breathed into them, and they begin to "come alive" in speech.

How that can occur may become clear to us when we enter a church. Its stained glass windows portray the biblical stories—perhaps the prodigal son, the raising of Lazarus, or the cross. These pictures speak to us. But if we walk around the exterior of the church, the pictures are gray and silent, and their message does not reach us. Only when we are inside do they begin to brighten up, to tell their story, to comfort and to judge. For the light that streams through them from outside fills them with color and illuminating power and life.

When the New Testament speaks of the Holy Spirit it refers to this miracle. Suddenly we no longer are standing outside, but we are within, where the words of the catechism which we thought to be dead all at once become usable, where they turn from stones into bread that feeds us, providing joy and the power to bear the burdens of each day.

But here too, as always, Jesus is concerned with more than a simple miracle in our personal life—in the "two-of-us" relationship between God and our soul. Our neighbor and the world around us are always included; for if anyone lets this life-giving Word become effective in him, "out of his heart shall flow rivers of living water." Jesus makes a point of seeing that the benefits are passed along. If anyone is interested only in spiritual enjoyment and pious self-edification, he allows the hoarded water of life to become a stagnant pool. For this water stays "living" only as long as it flows on and benefits someone else. Where Jesus Christ enters our life we become active; we cease to be centered on ourselves. Once his fire has begun to burn in us, it cannot remain hidden; it warms and enlightens the people with whom we come in contact. The city built on a hill cannot remain hidden.

Anyone whom this Spirit has brought to the light will, by his mere "being," drive away all darkness, shadiness, and gloom wherever he is. Much that is filthy or ambiguous just can't find room in his presence. He doesn't have to talk piously all the time, by any means. After all, it doesn't say "out of his 'mouth' shall flow living water"; but out of his "heart." That means it all will radiate from his being, his mere presence. And maybe people will be interested in hearing a *word* from a person like that. Haven't we known a person once who radiated all that, a person of whom we had to confess—long before we learned his confession—"We are glad that he is around"?

One pressing question, of course, must not be overlooked. It is a very honest question, and we Christians usually shove it aside. It goes like this: "Isn't the joy that we find in our relation to Christ seriously dampened and clouded if we see (or think we see) the territorial sovereignty of this Christ steadily shrinking as he is pushed more and more to the periphery of the world?" In church we sing pious hymns, and the ancient message rings from the high pulpit. But a few miles from here, where the waves of Asia lap at the shores of our own land, those songs and that proclamation *also* ring out (for this Lord has his islands and his beachheads in every ocean). But the tones seem to be drowned out by the cries of ideology and by tirades of hate, while around and among us the equally bad tide of indifference rises higher and higher. Can Christ still make us glad? That is the question. In the midst of a world of anxiety, can our thirst and our hope still be met through him, when we note that those forces which would choke him off and put him to silence grow ever stronger? I am not only referring, as I said, to the reign of ideological atheism, but also to our own territory, which seems to slip further and further from his grasp; to various journalists who mock him or silence him in their columns or secretly between the lines; to Easter parades with new hats and hullabaloo, instead of joy and exaltation of the Lord; to horoscopes and spiritualists, who have taken the place of the Holy Spirit; to the saying that what matters is the money and not the service—with all the devastating consequences that are washing away the foundations of our society.

Isn't it also the frightening signal of a defeat, the dangerous sign of a vacuum which the spirit of inhumanity is bound to absorb into itself little by little? What does it mean for us right now when we must admit, "I find peace of soul in Christ; a chorale does me good; I know what it means to find a liberated conscience because of him and to be able to come to him with everything that gives me concern. But what use are all these subjective and personal benefits of so-called piety, when it is no longer true that his kingdom really is coming and that all power is given to him in heaven and on earth? If *that* is no longer established, and the reins of the world have long since passed into other hands, isn't the comfort of piety simply empty sentimentality and perhaps only an ostrichlike approach to reality?"

All of that is by no means the bold question of our atomic generation alone; it already rings out in the message of the prophets. It constituted the hungering and the thirsting, the testing and the hoping of Israel. There too the question kept cropping up as to whether the boundaries of Israel were the boundaries of God, whether Egypt and Assyria didn't have other gods, and whether all of us therefore (Israel and Christianity) didn't worship a Western provincial god, whether in reality our faith was not a tightly limited, geographically and historically limited, ideology, and whether it was not therefore merely a matter of a Christian "sector" on the religious map.

If that were the case, then I would have to break off this attempt at preaching as quickly as possible. At best, I could try to enter the lists for a few humanitarian ideals and our Western "way of life." But I couldn't honestly proclaim the Lord of life and death, the God of grace and judgment.

Since the prophets of the Old Covenant knew of the critical question, they passionately protested against the shrunken and wrong-headed belief that their God was merely a local entity and that the history of the Gentiles had been withdrawn from his control. Even the Cushites, Egypt, and Assyria (Hos. 9:6) obey his nod, even if they have no inkling of the commanding arm they unwittingly follow. And if the other hemisphere, if the hostile nations with their idols and ideologies press in upon the people of God, if the red machine or even the self-serving of people in the Western welfare states decimates the little band of the pious until only a couple of old women crouch around the altars, then that is not a sign that God has lost the battle and is on his last legs; on the contrary, precisely then has he won his secret victory. Pharaoh, Nebuchadnezzar, and Mao Tse-tung are only lashes and scourges of judgment which he swings in his hand. Even the apocalyptic horsemen get their starting signal from *him*.

The atheistic regions are also marked on *God*'s map. And the red banners that signify the public displays of Communistic programs and also the erosion in our own world—those banners are raised by his hand. For the regions of atheism by no means indicate the areas where *man* has taken the reins into his own hands and where God has no more to say. They merely point out groups of men who are caught up in illusory dreams and who have no conception of *who* the Lord in the world's house actually is. It is God himself, therefore, who lets summit conferences break down or succeed. And it will be he alone who permits either a flood or a nuclear holocaust to come upon us.

God is not the monarch of the Western world, who keeps a couple of insignificant Christians as his bodyguard, while the major part of our planet is ruled by other, opposing Caesars who take delight in mocking his subjects. They also live and move and have their being in him, and when he takes away their breath, they are no more (Ps. 104:29). Stalin's stroke, racial conflicts, and ideological controversies are at his beck and call, and even the earthquakes in Chile and the convulsions of nature are, like fire, flame, and wind, servants of his. He uses these servants to jolt the whole earth into attention through judgments and shocks, through afflictions and signs of his majesty.

God certainly does not live because men believe in him. Even in prehistoric times before there were dinosaurs, to say nothing of human beings, his Spirit floated over the waters. And in the end, when everything is swallowed by the universal grave, he will walk among the tombs, still in control. *Men* rule by having followers. *God,* however, is also Lord of the dead planets where there is no one to recognize him. If the fabulous comes to pass, and he awakes men to faith, if he causes a light to dawn on them and lets them sense his love, if he comes among them in his Son, then he does those things, not because he wants to create a palace guard on earth, but because the wonder of his love occurs and because his heart seeks a "thou."

I believe that knowing all of this is a comfort and a joy; that there were people before us, patriarchs and prophets, worried by the same problems that we face. We are, in fact, *not* the first generation to be worried by looking at the globe and seeing the shrinking area that can be colored "Christian." It is comforting and cheering that we and our questions stand within the communion of saints so that we can see how the Father of faith, instead of removing these problems and worries, redeems us from them.

The hardest questions of life are never "removed" (we never learn why God does this or that, why a plane crashes or a mine disaster occurs). But we are "redeemed" from the destructive power of these questions. No longer can panic overwhelm us when we do not understand the meaning of what God permits to happen to us. No longer will his love puzzle us; we will learn to believe in that love even when we do not comprehend the means that love chooses to express itself.

Therefore we no longer look spellbound at the map in order to trace the advance of Antichrist with paralyzing dismay. What we see on the map with our natural eyes is deceptive, because it lets us see only the sandy sea of a wilderness in which God's footprints hopelessly disappear. Since Jesus has walked the earth, however, we are made worthy of more than a look at God's *feet*; now we may look into his *heart* and know that all things are held in him: the prostitutes and the Pharisees, the Christians and the atheists, America and Red China. It is just as Goethe intimated in his own way—that Orient and Occident rest in the peace of his hand and that no one can escape the Father's outspread arms.

Thus we know where the thirst of our questions will be quenched and where in the wilderness the true springs flow. Therefore, this story would tell us, put aside all prejudgments about whether good could come out of Nazareth and listen for once, unreservedly and fully awake, to his *Word*. See if something doesn't come to you then that you never held possible— neither in your most frightened moments nor in your keenest hopes. Bring him your hunger and your thirst, your anxiety and your boredom, your burdened conscience and your pride; then watch and see what happens—how everything leaves his presence changed. Perform an experiment with God and see how he reacts.

The intellectuals and "big-wigs" in our story, at any rate, continue on in the wrong direction. Perhaps they were all too secure and no longer knew hunger or thirst. The little people, however, were unprejudiced enough to hear the new sound. It was their thirst that sharpened their hearing for the bubbling of the spring, and they concluded in all simplicity, "No man ever spoke like this man!" He is, indeed, only a "man" to them, no more—not *yet*. Of course they did not grow up in the Christian West as we did. They only heard the bells ring without knowing where they were hanging. But they had caught a first breath of his Spirit. And now they can do nothing else than go after this spring, where they will burst into bloom. The wheel-spinning will come to an end. Life can begin again, for here is One who makes all things new.

15. WHAT IS THE "DEATH OF GOD" ALL ABOUT?

As he passed by, he saw a man blind from his birth.

And his disciples asked him, "Rabbi, who sinned, this man or his parents, that he was born blind?"

Jesus answered, "It was not that this man sinned, or his parents, but that the works of God might be made manifest in him."

John 9:1–3

This story revolves around the old question that we have discussed so often: why there is meaningless and tormenting suffering in the world—and how God can let it happen. It is not necessary for us to think about the mass deaths in Bangla Desh to have this question overwhelm us. A look at a traffic accident which tears a mother from her children is enough. One single case of multiple sclerosis is enough, or the sight of a cancer victim in the last stages of the disease suffices to throw into question our belief in a divine governance of the world and, even more, in a kindly Father in heaven.

A horrible event of which we are "eyewitnesses" is a reality. The God in whom we believe, however, has no reality of the sort to which we can be eyewitnesses. We trust an invisible One. Can this invisible One, however, stand up in competition with what we "see" in all its gruesomeness? Doesn't our observation, therefore, refute him?

That question was asked by Job long ago. And it may be a comfort to us that these modern questions which throw us into such anxiety are not new. The great believers of earlier days, the people of the Bible, have also had to cross these chasms. They too questioned the support of their life. They too cried out from vales of tears and out of the worry caused by horrors and injustices, while God seemed to be silent or absent.

The question of why there must be "suffering" in the world, and whether gods or men are responsible for it, is one of the oldest and toughest questions of mankind—and is apparently the hardest of them all. Both in the ancient tragedy of *Oedipus* by Sophocles and in the work of our contemporary, Albert Camus, it forms the central theme. And the question always involves a meaning which is not seen and yet which must be seen if we are to come to terms with suffering and find peace for ourselves once more.

It is not necessary, however, to think about extreme cases of suffering or torment in order to run up against this testing by meaninglessness. The treadmill of our daily routine, "the service of the eternally synchronized clock," are also areas from which springs the question of whether all that really ought to be, or whether it is not just a meaningless cycle in empty space. That is what Camus meant by saying, "Get up, streetcar, four hours' work, eat, sleep, Monday, Tuesday, Wednesday, Thursday, Friday, Saturday, always the same rhythm—for a long time that is a comfortable way. One day, however, the 'why' stands there, and in this disgust mixed with astonishment everything begins."

What begins? Camus means that through this question man really begins to be man. For in the same moment that he poses the question of "why" he no longer drifts along half-awake; he himself becomes the question. Now he begins to think over who in the world he is, what he is to do with himself, and what he is to make out of himself.

Today, however, there are a number of people and groups who would immediately comment that this wrestling with the meaning of suffering is only a gigantic hoax. Such questions of meaning would quickly become things of the past, if men changed the social structures with an eye to justice and righteousness. All problems about how God could permit such things would thus take care of themselves. Even the question of God itself would prove to be irrelevant as soon as man began to take this world into his own hands with energy and foresight.

I am afraid that this proposal is so obviously far from reality that it is doomed to failure from the start. Even if all the utopias should bring a perfect world into being (only assumed for the moment!), would wasted motion and meaninglessness really cease? Isn't it possible that the well-filled and programmed robots called "men" would freeze in the smoothly oiled action of the social machinery and, more than ever, pose Camus's question about the why and wherefore? And wouldn't the people, who even in a world of perfection (if such a thing is possible) are still "men after the fall," continue to suffer from one another? Wouldn't there be any more intrigues, self-seeking, envy, and aggressive drives? Even a Marxist philosopher like Herbert Marcuse has occasionally shown us that he knows something about that problem.

I fear that the question about why there is suffering and pain in the world, what it means, and how it can be brought into harmony with faith in a kind and almighty God will not stop being asked until Judgment Day. And no change in the world, no revolution, will be able to silence it.

This is the question with which our text begins. A man born blind is obviously a very striking instance of meaninglessness; an instance that brings discord into the symphony of creation and thereby compromises it. One lone way out of this humiliation of God seems still available. That would be to show that a sin had been committed, a sin which had entailed this blindness as "punishment."

There is a certain sense, in fact, in seeing suffering as punishment. And in that case the fate of the blind man would have been understandable. It would then appear to be just, and to that extent "justified." The people who ask the Lord this question, "Who sinned . . . that this man was born blind?" were intent on precisely this solution. This solution to the problem of suffering was, moreover, the common one for Jewish thought of that period. By looking for sin, they intended to save the reputation of divine righteousness.

Jesus, however, declined to get involved in the construction of such a connection between sin and fated suffering. According to him, one should not ask the question "why," or on what metaphysical grounds, this man has been afflicted with the fate of blindness. On the contrary, one must ask "to what end," that is, to what purpose have his eyes remained blind and without sight. In that case the answer is: He is blind so that

God's glory can become manifest in him. And that glory flashes forth in the Savior who meets him in this moment. He is, remember, the "light of the world." To see him, the dead eyes are awakened. The breath of resurrection touches even those whose eyes are dead. And if they are thus raised—raised by *him*—then these once dead eyes see miracles and graces that usually escape the notice of so-called healthy and normal eyes.

One sees the Lord only when one has gone through death and has been awakened by him. How many have heard him speak (with good ears!), and how many have seen his deeds (with healthy eyes!), and yet they have heard precisely *nothing*, nor have they seen anything. They inspect their new yoke of oxen, or they play poker with the boys, and everything is forgotten. Then when he is crucified, they may have savored the sensation, or wept sentimental tears. But they saw nothing of the tremendous display of God that was taking place before them. Their healthy eyes were kept shut, and their equally healthy human understanding did not react. The man who was once born blind but now can see, however—I imagine for a moment that he was present at Golgotha—found that dark event transparent. He once again recognized the One who had dawned upon him as the light of the world. And when the sun lost its radiance, he noted that in the darkness of the night on Golgotha the "sun of righteousness" began its course, and God set the work of redemption in motion. His renewed eyes were dazzled as the cross suddenly ceased to be a mere gallows and became instead the sign of supremacy of God's new world.

But what can this story mean to *us*? One thing could be that we no longer are to ask, "Why did that happen to me?" but that we ask instead, "For what purpose has God sent that to me?"

Is it really that simple to come to terms with the problem of suffering? Is a slight change in asking the question all it takes? Doesn't that verge on being a cheap trick?

In our story, it is true, the suffering of blindness was directed toward a quite definite end—toward that hour when the paths of this man and Jesus crossed, and the glory of God was revealed to him. But does that instance permit itself to be generalized so simply? Can one really say, then, that every plane crash, every death of a child by hunger or accident is good for "something" and therefore has its meaning? What meaning could that be? I am afraid that here we either start to stammer or we begin to speculate or just simply to mouth phrases.

And here again Camus has given the more honest answer (the name of this crusader for the absurd keeps forcing itself in upon our topic). For Camus has one of his characters, the physician, Dr Rieux, say, "I will refuse to my dying day to love a creation in which children are martyred." Where this horror occurs, we keep silence; every rational answer breaks down, and all becomes dark in the direction of our "To-what-purpose" question—even "theologically." A theology that has a prefabricated answer ready for everything is unbearable.

And didn't Jesus of Nazareth himself make a suggestion of this sort, a suggestion that would prohibit us from making a "teleology of suffering" out of this event as we sought to discern the purposeful "To what" in everything that happened? Didn't he say that the blindness of this man gained its meaning only in the encounter with him, the Savior; but that this was a special, almost exclusive event, and that afterwards the "night is coming, when no man can work . . ."?

Aren't we actually living through that night now, in the time after Christ, when it is no longer possible to discern what good can come out of the things that horrify us: criminal assaults on children, the Kennedy assassinations, the lonely decline of people in nursing homes, the deformity of thalidomide babies? But if the night has begun when no man can work against these things, and nobody is able to discover their meaning, then that night is a sort of dark side of God—a darkness in which God seems to vanish from us.

In that case, the night of meaninglessness becomes still darker and "the wasteland grows." That is what Nietzsche had his "madman" proclaim. And this idea that God is dead has run through many variations in modern intellectual history before and after Nietzsche.

In our generation there are even theologians who have

espoused this idea. To talk about "God," they say, is to talk about the "beyond," to talk "theistic metaphysics." The view in that direction, however, is gone. We are given the arrangement of what is "this side" of the beyond, the "here and now." At most, all that is left to us on the debris-strewn field of religion is the human figure of Jesus—he who took our human destiny upon his shoulders, remained with us in the God-forsaken "here and now" and by his great example conveyed to us a hint of what mankind could become, and a hint of the possibilities that lay within us.

"God is dead." That means that he is dead to us; he is absent; he has no more significance for us. The world is handed over to itself and its self-contained laws. That, and nothing else, is the reason for the existence of meaningless suffering and the blind dice-game of chance. That is also the reason why all attempts at forced meanings are doomed to failure and why they lead to illusion and a "poetic con game." In Jean Paul's great Death-of-God vision the dead children awake in their little graves and ask the Son of God, "Jesus, have we no Father?" And Jesus answers with streaming tears, "We are all orphans, you and I; we are without a Father." He was wrong, he tells them; there is no one. There is only "the numb, silent night," only "cold, eternal necessity," only "crazy chance."

Therefore the suffering of the man born blind—and especially the far greater suffering of the Jews gassed by the Nazis—has no sense either. It just arose from arbitrary, even coincidental intersections of causal chains. And for this reason (as was said during the Cologne Kirchentag in 1965) the hymn verse "who o'er all things so wondrously reigneth" cannot be sung after Auschwitz. What we have experienced is only an excess of insanity; God knows it is not "wondrous," nor is it a sign that anyone is "reigning" over us. Alone and forsaken, we have been handed over to the play of energy and matter. We are alone, as Jean Paul said, in the wide grave of the All.

Which one of us dares to say a word against this honest despair? Who from our conventional congregation is at all prepared even to take seriously this cry from the depths, this cry from the darkness of God? Shall we continue, untouched by it, to celebrate our liturgies while brothers and sisters right beside us are harassed by meaningless suffering, while the countenance of their Father in heaven disappears, and they still clutch with their last ounce of strength to the man Jesus of Nazareth?

The theoretical arguments which could be marshalled over against this vision of the void seem to stick in one's throat. Even the biblical answer to the riddle of human destiny, "What I am doing you do not know now, but afterward you will understand" (John 13:7)—even these words will hardly cross our lips. Couldn't the reference to an "afterward" when the meaning will reveal itself also be an illusion?

In my opinion only *one* person would have the right and the credentials to speak this "nevertheless" of faith, and to testify to the living God's presence—all wastelands of silence and all meaninglessness to the contrary. This one person, who could say it and from whom we could accept it, must be a Christian who has *himself* been able to sing the praise of God in the dark valley—in that moment when no fatherly visage seemed to gaze at him, but only the grimace of a soulless fate. Those who knew how to praise the living God as they entered the gas ovens or endured the tortures of the executioners—and not merely in stately cathedrals or in the framework of the middle-class Christian tradition—they *alone* have effectively dispelled the specter of the death of God, and have reduced it to empty words. From them alone could we still accept the phrase "who o'er all things so wondrously reigneth."

Have there ever been such "hymns from hell"? Have we testimony that one person saw the heavens open where others saw only a forsaken throne of God?

We know that Stephen (Acts 7:54 ff.) saw the heavens open as he was met by a hail of stones from his murderers, and that he saw his Lord at the right hand of God. It is said that, as he was giving the sermon which led to his execution, his face shone like that of an angel (Acts 6:15). Yet the murder of such a witness seems to be a direct refutation of God. Precisely the same testimony against the death of God has also been made in *our* time: in Auschwitz, Dachau, and Ravensbrück, and also in the Warsaw ghetto. In his memoirs, Carl Zuckmayer told about a Catholic priest in the Ravensbrück concentration camp who, when the whistle blew to awaken them every morning, sang the Gloria Patri in a loud voice that resounded over the whole camp—despite all the beating and torment he had to endure every day because of it. And in his biography Heinrich Grüber recounts a similar concentration camp scene: the chaplain of the camp, one who suffered with his comrades and comforted them, becoming a strong stay for that sorely tried fellowship, is taken off to execution—apparently the most senseless act of an already senseless situation. Wasn't this really a defiant refutation of God, a horrible testimony to his death? And in this abyss of forsakenness the Christians in the camp assemble secretly. They are not ashamed of their tears and their spiritual need, but they pray the fifty-sixth Psalm, which ends in a hymn of praise:

> Put thou my tears in thy bottle!
> Are they not in thy book? . . .
> This I know, that God is for me . . .
> in God I trust without a fear.
> What can man do to me?

Here, in reality, within the experience of divine silence, that praise and confession is given which people later will say is no longer possible after Auschwitz.

Who is right?

I believe that extreme situations release the special depths of truth that our faith possesses. Auschwitz and Ravensbrück *were* extreme situations. And under those circumstances God was praised. We should listen to this testimony of extremity.

The three astronauts, circling the moon in the awful emptiness of space, were in such an extremity. Meanwhile, on earth, in the midst of this cosmic oasis and its comfort, people were raving about how God's heaven had proven empty and how man's computers had taken over what once had been ascribed to God—the governance of the world. But those three space travelers, as they flew along far out in the universe, surrounded by lurking catastrophes, read in turn from the biblical creation story. "In the beginning God created the heavens and the earth." They read all seven days of creation, and many of us heard their voices from space. Another time the captain of the spacecraft said a prayer for his congregation on earth and for Christmas peace. As he said "Amen," he was joined by a loud "Amen" from the men at the command and control equipment in NASA's space center. Last year I was in Houston myself, where I talked with the astronauts, physicists, technicians, and space doctors of NASA. I know from those conversations that the unison "Amen" which affirmed that prayer from space was no empty phrase. On the contrary, I consider that conversation between heaven and earth to be an impressive glorification of God and an overwhelming testimony against his supposed death. I know people who were moved by it.

In the void of space, therefore, and in the midst of martyrdom by senseless death and murder, that testimony ascends to heaven in confidence that God hears, even though he is silent; and that he is at work, even when the world seems to have been put on its own. Job says of God that he gives songs in the night (Job 35:10). In this case the "night" is that incomprehensible fate that could almost make us get the wrong idea about God. Not only the cry for help, but also the song of praise comes out of the depths. It even comes from the fiery furnace of Nebuchadnezzar (Dan. 3).

But is this rising out of the depths of suffering to God, this song of praise by which we soar above the harassment of the present situation, possibly only a sort of cowardly escape, a bit of religious opium-smoking, so to speak, that we talk ourselves into because we would collapse without the support of such a faith, unable otherwise to endure a life without consolation?

In the light of the testimony out of extremity which I have just cited, this question is admittedly hard. Could one really, sitting in that deep dark hole, have the strength, to say nothing of the desire, to make up a father who lived above the stars? Wouldn't that just mean adding an extra burden—the burden, in addition to everything else, of standing up under the blunt contradiction between this "theistic father-figure" and the

215

extremely unfatherly insanity which is inflicted upon one? Wouldn't it be much easier to play dead like an animal, bearing the blind play of chance like a cynic or a hero? In my own experience I have never known a person who sat in a dark hole to reach out for such religious inventions of fantasy. On the other hand, I *have* known many people who, in times of war or disaster, gave themselves up to fatalism and murmured the word "destiny" as the beam of destruction hit them.

Obviously something totally different occurs when a person sings "songs in the night," when he has learned to say in the darkness of congenital blindness or even in danger of terror or hunger, "Nevertheless I am continually with thee" (Ps. 73:23). When someone is in a position to do that, you may be sure of one thing: he has *already* had his experience with God, and in a quite *different* way. For he may have learned from Jesus who this God is: that he seeks out the lost in their far country; that he bears in love and sadness, all scorn and every rejection that men heap upon him; that he is, indeed, a God of the darkness who does not permit himself to be grasped easily, like a fetish or an idol; a God who staged the riddle of Golgotha, permitting his Son to die forsaken, and at the same time was present in that darkness so that the crucified One could finally bow his head in peace.

Anyone who has experienced God in this way, in the figure of Jesus, will certainly look to him and call out to him when he must pass through the floods of tribulation and meaninglessness. For he now bears a certainty in his heart which is not of this world and which therefore cannot be taken from him by anything that occurs in it. Admittedly, he doesn't know the meaning of the dark providences that come upon him. In this respect he is confronted with nothingness exactly as any atheist would be. He will even forbid himself from tinkering around with attempts to find meaning because it appears to him to be pride to want to know what is reserved to God alone. No, he doesn't see any meaning either, *but* he believes and trusts in him who does know the meaning. Therefore, he simply puts everything he has into that trust, because in Jesus Christ he has seen into the heart of God himself. In that glimpse he discovers that this heart is brimful of love, of love that comes down to the manger of Bethlehem and to the cross of Golgotha, to the hungering and thirsting, to the humble and the offended, and to the wounded conscience. At the same time he sees that this love of God is a concealed, or, as Luther said, a "love hidden beneath the cross." It is a love, therefore, that does not lie cheaply or easily to hand. Faith must hold fast to it in the darkness in order to experience it in an overpowering way.

If that, however, is true, then a promise awaits us precisely in pain and suffering, and even in the experience of meaninglessness and the absurd. Precisely this darkness, precisely this confusion of the lines, can incline us to turn our gaze upon the heart of all things, bringing us certainty and comfort from the only place they are to be found: the One and Only of whom the Christmas carol sings,

> This little child, of lowly birth,
> Shall be the joy of all the earth.[1]

This may account for the fact that all great men of faith have also been sufferers; that they were confronted by the black wall and the void, and that they made it through the most difficult crises of faith until they finally experienced the very thing which had driven them to despair as a visitation—a gracious visit. And it may also account for the opposite fact that people who live in unbroken and well-filled affluence are often the cheated ones. Their life knew no depths out of which they could learn to call for help. Therefore there is a hospital chaplaincy, but no playboy or cocktail party chaplaincy.

Is it therefore really permissible to talk about the death of God? Isn't it more likely to be the exact opposite: that we ourselves have died and must be awakened out of our death? We are surrounded by sheer promises of life, and the promise of the Lord, "I am with you always, even to the end of the world," is still in force. But do we want to be with him? He knocks, but do we open? Everything depends on the answer to that question.

1. Martin Luther, "From heaven above to earth I come."

Not long ago a book appeared by the Czech Communist Vitezslav Gardavsky called *God Is Not Quite Dead.* Here is a book where someone speaks about religion and atheism out of the thought-world of dialectic materialism. He calls himself an atheist and is convinced that he is one. But this Marxist reads the Bible. He reads it impartially, somewhat inquisitively. He is in no way encumbered by any sort of Christian tradition. Since he reads the Bible through Marxist glasses—exactly as the Greeks and Jews and ancient Germans had their special glasses in their time—often wondrous, sometimes even fascinating perspectives come to light. One might say it amounts to a disengagement from the Bible, which can provide totally new impacts on the understanding. "This book," meaning the Bible, "will be difficult to forget completely," he says, "and mankind can hardly ever become completely indifferent to it." And another time: The Bible "must be counted among those books . . . which one must have read if he does not want to be poorer than other people."

Thus the eternal Word contained in this book began its history with Gardavsky—a history set in motion, as always, by a higher hand whenever anyone is ready to become involved.

Judged from a confessional standpoint, it is true that some amazing gaps and deviations appear, which could shock a Christian. But what about it? Perhaps the situation here is similar to what we concluded about the story of the woman with a hemorrhage—the woman was caught, we said, in the conceptual framework of magic. And so, in accordance with magical practices, she tried to produce physical contact with Jesus by touching his robe with her finger. In that way she hoped for a transfer of power—a most unchristian idea. But the Lord was broad-minded, and completely undoctrinaire. He accepted this person who sought the way to him from quite heathen regions.

Gardavsky too—and this is where I see the parallel—asks about biblical truth from a quite unchristian angle, in this case out of a Marxist system of thought. But he too has touched the figure of Jesus, exactly like that woman in Mark, on the hem of his robe. He does not yet stand eye to eye with the Christ, nor does he answer him—not yet!—with a christological confession as the church does. He approaches, again like that woman, from behind. Will the story continue as in the New Testament: The Lord turns and asks, "Who touched me?" and makes himself known to this person? I often ask myself these days what it means when, at the turn of the seventh decade in the twentieth century, a Marxist, of all people, begins to discover the Bible. Here is a man who doesn't come out of the game sanctuary of Western Christianity, but from an area which has been thoroughly disinfected against Christian bacteria, and he now draws the preliminary conclusion, "God is not quite dead; I have detected some sort of life. And now I am staying on the trail of this life I have thus sensed." What does it mean, I ask myself, that an atheist thus sets out on the trail of life, while representatives of an unbroken Christian tradition talk about the death of God? How remarkable it all is, and what lies behind it?

It is a sign of hope. That is why this book has stirred me so. A Marxist barks, because a call has reached him. And even if this bark is still not a prayer, at least in the framework of practical Christian understanding, it certainly will be accepted in heaven. Here someone has been called by his name, and the continuation, "Thou art mine" (Isa. 43:1), no longer lies within our power. But even this last word could already have been spoken in eternity, because God is more broad-minded than the dogmatic pencil-pushers of Christianity, above all greater than our hearts.

The Lord who said of himself, "I am the light of the world" touched a man born blind and made him see. Gardavsky too was born in a world which was screened off from that light. And nevertheless one of its beams has found its way to him, and he rubs his eyes in amazement.

> The Sun that warms and lights us;
> By his grace he doth impart
> Eternal sunshine to the heart;
> The night of sin is ended![2]

2. Martin Luther, "Christ Jesus lay in death's strong bands."

This hymn of praise from those who could shake off the curse of darkness and the terror of the void sounds through the whole history of faith. It is not the sated and the secure who experience this miracle, but those who "sit in darkness and in the shadow of death." *They* discern the signals of God. That is not a matter of recognizing higher worlds or of similar religious and metaphysical things. It concerns the power of liberation which shatters our chains here and now, putting our life on a new and certain basis.

Thus the story of the man born blind invites us to take a chance with him who can call for graves to open and for dead eyes to see. The air is full of promise.